The Philosophy Of Shankara
- Primary Source Edition

Buch, Maganlal A.*

Nabu Public Domain Reprints:

You are holding a reproduction of an original work published before 1923 that is in the public domain in the United States of America, and possibly other countries. You may freely copy and distribute this work as no entity (individual or corporate) has a copyright on the body of the work. This book may contain prior copyright references, and library stamps (as most of these works were scanned from library copies). These have been scanned and retained as part of the historical artifact.

This book may have occasional imperfections such as missing or blurred pages, poor pictures, errant marks, etc. that were either part of the original artifact, or were introduced by the scanning process. We believe this work is culturally important, and despite the imperfections, have elected to bring it back into print as part of our continuing commitment to the preservation of printed works worldwide. We appreciate your understanding of the imperfections in the preservation process, and hope you enjoy this valuable book.

Presented to the
LIBRARY *of the*
UNIVERSITY OF TORONTO
by
Professor R. F. McRae

*The Gaekwad Studies
in
Religion and Philosophy : VI*

THE
PHILOSOPHY OF SHANKARA

Printed at the Vidya Vilas Press, Baroda
and published by A. G. Widgery,
the College, Baroda.
31-3-1921

THE PHILOSOPHY OF SHANKARA

The Sujna Gokulji Zala Vedanta Prize Essay

By

Maganlal A. Buch, M. A.
Author of 'Zoroastrian Ethics' and
'The Spirit of Ancient Hindu Culture.'

BARODA.

(All rights reserved by the Author)

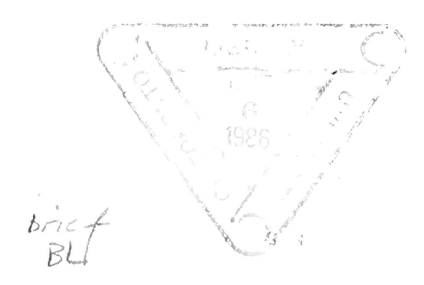

brief
BL

To,

His Excellency Manubhai Nandshanker Mehta, C. S. I., M. A, LL. B.

The Diwan, Baroda State.

I humbly dedicate this book as a mark of respect for one to whom I owe my first impulse to the study of our Hindu Philosophy.

M. A. BUCH.

CONTENTS

Preface ... ... pp
Abbreviations ... ...
Introduction 1–16
Chapter I. Eastern and Western Philosophy: Their Starting-points, Methods, and Results 17–40
Chapter II. Shankara's attitude towards other opposed systems ... 41–63
Chapter III. Metaphysics ... 64–107
Chapter IV. The Doctrine of Maya 108–128
Chapter V. Ethical conceptions in Adwaitism 129–174
Chapter VI. A Comparison of Shankara's System with some Modern Philosophies 175–217
Chapter VII. How far is Shankara's System a Philosophy in the modern sense of the term? Shankara's Epistemology 218–276

PREFACE.

The present volume aims at supplying a cheap, popular exposition of the greatest Philosopher of India. It is admitted on all hands that Shankaracharya has the greatest following in India and his memory is highly cherished by countrymen. I, therefore, found it necessary to systematise his teachings and to make his thought accessible to a lay reader. The greatest authority on the subject undoubtedly is Dr. Deussen's thoroughgoing book. But his work is costly and bulky, and hence not so easily accessible as it should be. Further, it is my conviction that the great German scholar has failed to do justice to certain parts of Shankara's teachings, especially his theory of knowledge. This was due to the fact that he was too much obsessed by Kantian teaching. It was also necessary to bring out the significance of Shankara's teaching in the History of Philosophy, and this can be best done by a detailed comparison of his theory with some modern philosophies. The fact, however remains that " the last word on Shankara's philosophy is not said as yet. " Hence if this volume proves a stimulus to other thinkers to appreciate Shankara, the author's labour will be amply rewarded.

Baroda MAGANLAL A. BUCH.
March, 1921

ABBREVIATIONS.

S. B. Shankara Bhashya.
Bg. C. Commentary on the Gita.
Br. C. Commentary on Brihadaranyaka.
H. C. Commentary on Hastamalkiya.
Ma. C. Commentary on Mandukya.
Ai. C. Commentary on Aitareya.
Ta. C. Commentary on Taittiriya.
Kath. Up. Katha Upanishad.
Ch. Up. Chandogya Upanishad.
Mu. Up. Mundaka Upanishad.

INTRODUCTION.

The earliest germs of the Adwaita doctrine are to be found in the Vedas. The ancient seers boldly grasped the conception of unity and gave it diverse expression in the Vedic hymns. " Of the one existence, the sages speak in diverse ways. " (Rg. 1. 164). The famous नासदीय hymn marks the dawn of philosophic speculation in India. In the Shatapatha Brahmana we read: " This soul is everything. " (S. Br. 2. 2, 1.). The Upnishads, however, for the first time, do substantial justice to these thoughts. The germs of the highest idealism are to be found there. The human spirit takes its boldest flights in the speculation of the Upnishads. All the main ideas of Shankara's theory are anticipated by the Upnishadic seers. Now the Adwaita may be briefly summarised in the following propositions : (1) Brahman is the only Reality; (2) Atman is the same as Brahman; (3) The empirical world is unreal or illusory; (4) There are two kinds of Brahman set forth; the higher and the lower, this corresponds to the distinction between Brahman and Ishwara or God of the religious consciousness. Now we will see that there are ample quotations in the Upnishads to support all these contentions. "In the beginning, Dear, there was Sat (Existence, Reality) only—One only without a second." (Ch. Up.). When the ultimate Reality is referred to, sometimes Atman and sometimes Brahman is spoken of.

No duality, no Other exists in the final reality; all not-Brahman is unreal. The last distinction which seems to be ultimate in consciousness, between the subject and the object vanishes. The knower cannot be known. Atman is the one goal of philosophy; it is the reality *par excellence.* "Atman is to be seen, heard, understood, meditated, O Maitreyi; by seeing, hearing, understanding, and realizing Atman, all this world is known." (Br. Up. II. 1. 5). Atman or the ultimate self-consciousness is the key to the structure of Reality; it being known, all else becomes necessarily known. Atman is the one fact, making all else possible; it is the source of all sensation, all thought, all knowledge.

All these passages irresistibly point to the conclusion that Atman is the only reality, and that Atman is Brahman. " Self below, above, behind, right and left—Self is all this." (Ch. Up. VII. 25. 2.). " He who dwells in all beings, and within all beings whom all beings do not know, whose body all beings are, and who rules all beings within; he is thy Self, the ruler within, the Immortal." (Br. Up. III. 7. 15). " He is the one God, hidden in all beings, all-pervading, the Self within all beings, watching over all works, dwelling in all beings, the witness, the perceiver, the only one, free from qualities." (Ch. Up. VI. II.) These quotations are sufficient to establish the Upnishadic origin of the highest idealism of the Adwita-Vada, which boldly declares that the Self is the only Reality, that the Self and the Absolute are identical.

From these positions it follows that all

the empirical existence is mere Maya, mere illusion. "As O good one, by (the knowledge of) one ball of earth everything of the the nature of earth is known; the change (or modification) is an extension of words, a mere name; only the earth is true." (Ch. Up. VI. I. 4.). The supreme reality therefore belongs to the Absolute, the One; all else is shadow, mere appearance, mere name. " Only by the mind this is to be obtained; there is no multiplicity here whatsoever; he goes from death to death who sees any multiplicity-here." (Kath. Up. II. 4. 11). The word इव *as it were*, is so often used in connection with the realities extraneous to the Self, thereby implying the unreality of all that. "Where there is something else, *as it were;* " " where there is duality, *as it were;* " " Atman thinks *as it were*, moves *as it were.* " Even Dr Thibeaut has to say : " I am ready to admit that not impossibly these ' Iva's indicate that the thought of the writer who employed them was darkly labouring with a conceptionakin although much less explicit than the Maya of Shankara."

The distinction between the lower and the higher Brahman, the *para* and the *apara vidya*, the esoteric metaphysics, and exoteric doctrine, of which Shankara made so much use in unifying the texts of the Upnishads was no mere invention of that philosopher, but was a part of the Upnishadic doctrine. There are frequent references to two types of existence, the transcendental and the empirical in the Upnishads variously mentioned as Bhuman and Alpa and soon. "That is Brahman which you know thus, not this which you thus worship." "In the beginning Dear, there was Sat (Reality) only—One only without a second." Now corresponding to this distinction of existences is the distinction between two types of knowledge. The Para Vidya or transcendental philosophy leads to liberation; the Apara Vidya covers all empirical knowledge. (Mu. Up. I. 4. 5.)

The teaching of the Gita on the highest Reality, on God, man, and nature is substantially the Adwaita teaching. All other elements are completely sub-ordinate. The fact, therefore, that there is an admixture of Sankhya and Yoga in it, is a matter of little importance. The services of these different theories are enlisted in the support of the main doctrines of the Gitakar; but the Gitakar is very far from participating in the views of the Sankhya and Yoga as regards their views on the ultimate problems of metaphysics. Similarly, the question whether Karma or Bhakti or Gnana is the essential part of the teaching of the Gita belongs rather to the ethics than the metaphysics of the subject. The unity and harmony of the philosophical theory of the Gitakar remains therefore unaffected by these controversies.

Take first the conception of God in the Gita. There are two main aspects in which this conception is revealed to us. These correspond to the Saguna and Nirguna Brahman of Shankara. God is now represented as व्यक्त, and now represented as अव्यक्त. Which is the higher aspect of these two?

Shankara believes that the religious demands of an unevolved humanity requires that there should be the conception of a 'personal' God. But from the point of view of the Absolute, it has no existence. The Gita maintains the same view. The Gitakar says that there are two ways of approaching the Deity; the worship of the Avyakta God is very difficult for ordinary people. There is a clear assertion of the superiority of the Avyakta aspect of God. It is said that only the stupid consider God to be Vyakta; they fail to perceive His highest Avyakta aspect which is beyond the Vyakta aspect. (Bg. VII. 24). It is repeated very often that the idea of a personal God is due to Maya (Bg. VII. 25.).

Now how does God affect the other two factors man and the universe ? First, let us take the conception of जगत् or the world. It is variously called Maya, Prakriti, Swabhava, Kshetra. It may be rendered into English as the objective aspect of existence. To translate Prakriti by matter is to create confusion. Prakriti is not mere lifeless matter, but includes all the intellectual, emotional and volitional phenomena as well. " The great elements, Ahankara (egoism), Buddhi (willing) and the Avyakta (the principle connected with Buddhi), the ten senses, and the one mind, and the five objects of sense; desire and hatred, pleasure and pain, the aggregate; intelligence, firmness; this here described in brief, is the Kshetra with its modifications. " (Bg. XIII. 6-7). All the paraphernalia of consciousness, inner and outer, are thus gross matter; the principle of life, of intelligence, of activity is not in them; they are mere objects for a subject; mere instruments through which the soul works, having no existence in their own right.

The inner principle is called Kshetragna or the soul in man. He is the subject, the central source of all activity and knowledge, the one permanent, changeless factor in the midst of all change and destruction. Now, all experience, all knowledge, all existence presupposes the operation of these two factors the subject and the object. Take away either the subject or the object and the world vanishes. The object has no existence at all apart from the subject; the subject has no empirical existence apart from the object. " Whatever is born, whether unmoving or moving, know that to be from a commingling of Kshetra and Kshetragna." (Bg. XIII. 27.) The subject-aspect and the object-aspect of experience are there eternally; the former rendering possible the pleasure-pain experiences of the conative agent and the latter rendering possible the succession of cause and effect. (Bg. XIII. 20-21). Now the Gita recognises that the soul has two sides; it is subject of knowledge and ignorance, of pleasure and pain, of activity or passivity with reference to the empirical world or the object; in itself it is above all appearance, thought and change. (Bg. II. 25) It becomes entangled in the empirical life under the influence of the illusion of Prakriti. (Bg. XIII. 22).

The investigation of the essential nature of Atman or Kshetragna leads us to the relation it and God. The following description of Atman makes it clear that it is a transcendental reality. "It is ever-lasting, all-pervading, stable, firm, and eternal. It is said to be unperceived, to be unthinkable, to be unchangeable." (Bg II. 23. 25) Now according to the definition of the Real in the Gita, there can be only one Infinite, one Reality, one transcendental existence, "Of the unreal there is no existence; of the Real there is no non-existence: the true nature of both has been found out by seers of truth." (Bg. II. 16). All reality is time-less; all things that exist in time are unreal. Prakriti is, therefore, unreal; it has no absolute, ultimate, transcendental existence. But the soul is real being timeless; or it is timeless, because it is real. Now it is expressly laid down that the soul is nothing but the immanent existence of God in man. "Know Kshetragna to be Me, in all Kshetras." (Bg. XII. 3).

The identity of the individual soul and the supreme soul is quite emphatically asserted. " This undecaying supreme soul, being beginningless and void of Gunas, though seated in body, neither acts, nor is defiled by acts." (Bg. XIII. 31). Prakriti is really responsible for actions. (Bg. XII. 29).

The Kshetragna is not supremely real as Kshetragna; in its essence it is real. As an individual soul, as a subject, it has a one-sided, abstract existence; hence it has no reality. " Since I transcend the Becoming and also the Being, in the world and in the Veda, I am proclaimed the supreme spirit " (Bg. XV. 16-18). The Absolute is that in which all partialities, all one-sidedness, all incoherences are corrected and unified in a final, synthetic Reality; in which the subject relation is as much transcended as the object relation. Of course, both the subject and object, Kshetra and Kshetragna are mere manifestations of the Absolute: Maya or Prakriti has no existence and individual soul also has no existence apart from Brahman. The unreality of Maya in the Gita is bound up with the unreality of the individual soul as well as God; all these are alike objectively real; but as absolute beings they have no reality.

The one thinker who influenced Shankara most was Gaudapada. He is one of the greatest teachers of the Advaita doctrine and he deserves the credit of boldly identifying himself with the Advaita tradition of the Upnishads completely, to the exclusion of all other systems. Hitherto few had cared to disengage the Advaita theory from the mass of speculations in the Upnishads; few had tried to follow the logic of thought implicit in the scattered Adwaita theories laid down in the previous writings. This bold step was taken by Gaudapada.

Gaudapada maintains that there is no more reality in the waking life than the experiences of dreams. The first is external; the second is internal; but both agree in one point, their capability of being seen or being presented as objects. Both are believed to be real on this ground; but as the dream-experiences prove illusory after they are over; so also must be the case with the experiences of waking life. The true criterion of reality therefore is not the capability of becoming objects for a subject; but the capacity of persistence for all time. The test of reality is its persistence. But the experiences of waking life have both beginning and end, like such other illusions as dreams or mirage; hence they are no more real than the latter. (II. 6). Now it is said that the pragmatic test is satisfied in the case of waking life inasmuch as our experiences are verified by facts; here tangible things are used as means for tangible ends; we get actual satisfaction from food and drink. This test is not operative in the case of dreams. The सप्रयोजनता is the main difference between the two. Gaudapada replies that the experiences of a man who has quenched his thirst or hunger are stultified when he enters dream-life; a hungry man often appears as a man of satiated appetite and *vice versa*. Hence there is no advantage as regards सप्रयोजनता on either side. In both cases the reality has no existence beyond that particular state, be it of waking or dreaming. The difference lies merely in the instruments of cognition. What is then the substrate behind these illusions. ? It is Atman in both cases. Atman posits the illusion both of the subject and the object through the power of Maya. The whole cosmos is a result of this illusion. Virtually, " there is no dissolution, no creation, none in bondage, no pupilage, none desirous of liberation, none liberated. " (II. 32.) This is the final truth about the universe. No such thing as the universe, with all the variety and diversity it involves, exists. Every individual soul, every monad is responsible for his own cosmos. His world is his imagination. Really speaking, the world is like an illusion, a dream, or a castle in the air (II. 31). It has no existence, dependent or independent. (II. 34).

Reality is defined as that which is unchangeable. The true nature of a thing is the constant, permanent, immutable element in it. (III. 21). Evolution is a category which is inapplicable to the absolute truth or reality. If we once grant the reality of distinction, anything becomes anything, and there will be chaos. Hence that which is immortal can never pass into birth and death. (III. 19-22). All becoming, all change, all causality is an illusion, valid only in the empirical world and not in the transcendental sphere. (III. 25, 27). The reality of the empirical world is mind-dependent; the concept is responsible for our experience of the world. (:III. 31. 38). The philosophy of the Absolute which thus asks us to surrender all individual existence, experience, activity, demands of us very heavy sacrifices; the complete freedom from all relations, all conditions, all limitations which it promises, staggers the imagination of all but the most robust of us. (III. 39).

THE PHILOSOPHY OF SHANKARA

CHAPTER 1

EASTERN AND WESTERN PHILOSOPHY

Their Standpoints, Methods and Results

It has been said by one of the Western *savants*, who was very successful in placing himself in a kind of deep, sympathetic touch with the best thought of the East, that the Hindus were, above all, a nation of Philosophers. This dictum – very remote from the absurd talk of Macaulay – has a significance which requires to be brought out a little. The point of the compliment does not lie so much in the extensiveness and range, or the subtlety and depth of native philosophic speculation, as in the enormous influence which philosophic thought has exercised upon the Hindu mind. Some other nations have produced philosophers of equal calibre, have produced equally brilliant analyses of mind and soul and equally profound theories about the Infinite and the finite, about God, man and nature. But nowhere else was philosophy so little an academic affair and so much an actual living force ; nowhere else did it tinge so much the everyday life of the people. The reasons for this phenomenon lie in certain special characteristics developed by Hindu thought. We will here briefly bring out these peculiarities which give a distinguishing colour to all Hindu theories of life and conduct.

The Hindu mind, under the influences of the Eastern climate and environment has always shown an enormous fascination for abstract, mystical speculation about the immensities, eternities and infinities, confronting us. Hence the luxuriant growth of religions and philosophies in the East. A Hindu is more at home in the Infinite than in the finite, more at home in the timeless, spaceless world of pure spirit than in the

' cribbed, cabined and confin'd' world which lies about us. The Infinite alone is his centre of energy, his source of inspiration and the fountainhead of reality for him. All facts that can be branded as temporal or spatial are of ' the earth, earthy'. How can man indeed rest peacefully, contentedly in any state, of whose existence and nature he is not assured from day to day or even from century to century?

Thus we are brought to one of the fundamental differences in Western and Oriental philosophy. The impulse propelling different philosophies is often very different. The secret spring of the inner movement of thought in every case largely explains a good deal in subsequent developments. It is very important, therefore, to know the ultimate spring, the fundamental impetus of the philosophic mind in ancient India. This will at once unify the different systems of philosophy in India and will serve to differentiate them broadly from the rival systems which originated elsewhere. It will also give us the standpoint of our system—the principle which helps to explain everything peculiar in it.

Aristotle says that all philosophy begins in wonder. "Apart from man no being wonders at its own existence. When man first becomes conscious he takes himself for granted as something needing no explanation. But not for long, for, with the rise of the first reflexion, that wonder begins which is the mother of metaphysics and which made Aristotle say that men now and always seek to philosophise because of wonder".[1] All metaphysics is thus to a certain extent an offspring of wonder ; and the sages of the *Upanishads* often asked in sheer bewilderment and curiosity such questions as " Who am I ? " " Whence came this world ? " and so on. But this is not a complete explanation of the origin of the Hindu philosophy. The Hindu philosophers did not turn to philosophic speculation merely to satisfy the metaphysical itching of asking the why of

---

1. Schopenhauer : "The World as Will and Idea." Appendix 17.

things. The metaphysical impulse of Hindus had a deeper origin than the mere intellectual curiosity which seeks the ultimate roots of things and tries to peep "behind the veil". Nor was it in words of W. James, the "sentiment of rationality", which was striving to find satisfaction in philosophy. That is to say, Hindu philosophy did not come to birth as some philosophies in the West did, to satisfy the passion for order, system, coherence, consistency, wholeness in our thoughts about things. This had its fair share in the business, but it was not fundamental. The passion for unification, for systematisation was keen among the *Pandits* of the East, as among the *Pandits* of the West, but this does not give us the clue we want.

Again, some philosophers seek metaphysics to provide a safe basis of conduct for moral life; in such cases the ethical motive is ultimate and metaphysics is but a secondary product of what may be primarily an ethical need. Such was the case with Lotze.

But the Hindus did not attach so much importance to ethical problems of man's life as to make these the driving forces of his whole life. Nor was the Hindu system a response to a stirring need of providing secure foundations for sciences and reconciling the conflict of science and religion. Kant's great system was largely a product of such a need. Modern western philosophy began with doubt – doubt about everything in man and nature. Hence its predominantly epistemological character. The ancient Greek philosophy went straight to the object and healthily took it for granted that the human reason was quite competent to know the truth. But the searching spirit of the modern world questioned everything and above all, it questioned the capacity of human reason to grasp adequately the final truth about the fundamental constitution of reality. We therefore find philosophy turning itself into an inquiry into the limits and validity of human knowledge in the great idealistic philosophies since the time of Berkeley. The

Hindu seers were different from both; they had not complete confidence in the power of reason to know everything; but they were not quite so much obsessed by epistemological difficulties, as the modern philosophers.

It was in response to a practical need that Hindu philosophy arose. It was the all-powerful necessity to seek deliverance from the pettinesses, troubles, sufferings of this finite existence, which drove the Eastern sages to devise theories of life, offering a permanent, final escape from the taint of finiteness and a lasting place of refuge for the misery-stricken souls of the world. Within us there is an innermost need for rest which demands satisfaction. It is a need " to rise above the struggle for existence, to be freed from all change and opposition, from all ' doubleness ' and difference. Difference entails suffering, change, unrest, and this suffering and unrest cause man to aim at better conditions; but those attained, still more cruel disappointments await him. This whole process of oscillation must therefore be checked and suspended. Only in the eternal and immutable state after which we long, can this cease. But since all ideas arise in the world of experience, so unrestful and so much at the mercy of difference, no expression of ours can characterise positively the eternal and immutable state after which we long. And since all change and movement, when once we have attained this state is seen to be an illusion, we shall see that the longing for it is also an illusion. We must cease to be freed from all striving."² Such is the fundamental impulse of the oriental mind seeking rest,—final, absolute rest in the bosom of the changeless and the eternal. " इह हि सर्वस्य अन्तो: सुखं मे भूयाद्दुःखं मे मा भूयात् इति स्वरसत एव सुखोपादित्साद्दुःखजिहासे भवत: । तत्र यःकश्चित् पुण्यातिशयशाली अवश्यंभाविदुःखाविनाभूतत्वादनित्यत्वाच्च विषयजं सुखं दुःखमेवेति ज्ञात्वा यत्नेन ससाधनात्संसारात्यक्तासक्तिरत्यन्तं विरज्यते । विरक्तश्च संसारहानौ यतते । "³ This passage sets forth the essentially transitory and painful nature

---

2. Hoffding: Philosophy of Religion. p. 127.
3. H. Introduction.

of all worldly pleasures and the consequent necessity of rooting out worldly impulses. " न तृष्णायां सत्यां सुखस्य गंधमात्रमप्युपपद्यते । " Not a shadow of happiness is possible as long as the striving – the desire in us is not rooted out.[4]

Philosophy in India seeks to root out the very source of unrest in us, the very cause of all movement within. " अस्य अनर्थस्य हेतोः प्रहाणाय......सर्वे वेदान्ता आरभ्यन्ते । "[5] Here the philosophy of the East offers a very great contrast to the philosophy of the Greeks. The Greeks took the world to be a place of rest and happiness and did not think seriously that life was essentially miserable. " For he who enjoys the day of life with childlike Hellenic simplicity, however high a flight his genius may take in other respects, will only touch in passing the last and the highest problems of being, as did the Greeks; to seize them fully and clearly requires a deep feeling of the vanity and nothingness of all this life and a corresponding longing to pass *from the non-existent to to the existent,*

---

1. Bg. C. 2. 66.   5. S. B. Introduction.

from darkness to light, from death to immortality,' a longing by which the Indians were inspired even in ancient times, and which remained the true motive principle of their philosophy."[6]

From this fundamental standpoint follow many other characteristics of Eastern philosophy. Hegel has remarked that among Hindus, religion and philosophy were largely mixed up together, so that Hindu philosophies were rather theologies than systems of metaphysics. This statement contains an element of truth. In the first place, such a marked differentiation of the divergent departments of thought which has taken place in recent times was not known to the people in ancient India. Secondly, the fundamental motive of religion and philosophy is the same, although the ways by which each seeks it are different. Thirdly, the pioneers of religion and philosophy in India were generally the same; Shankara or Ramanuja, unlike Kant or Hegel are as much

---

6. Dr. Deussen p. 82.

teachers of religious truth as philosophers. Fourthly, the Hindu philosophers did not question the authority of the *Vedas*, but took revelation more or less as the basis of their thought. But above all, for the Hindus, philosophy was not a luxury of speculation, an outgrowth of wild intellectual activity, an efflorescence of the searching spirit of man in its highest form, but an affair of life. Like Rudolf Eucken, the Hindu thinkers thought of the fundamental importance of the problem of life, and philosophy as its handmaid. Hindu philosophy is, therefore, essentially a philosophy of life, on the right understanding of which depend the eternal interests of man. Hence the *Vedanta* is as much a part of Hindu religion and Hindu life, as of Hindu thought; it is of immense practical importance to all Hindus. This explains the theologic character of much of Hindu speculation.

The general conclusions to which the movement of thought led the most characteristic Eastern philosophers presents also a remarkable contrast to the results of the modern philosophic thought in the West. The most fundamental difference lies in the attitude towards the world or empirical existence. Modern thought, hence modern philosophy, is very much under the tyranny of the view-point of science. Hence it strives to make room in a system of metaphysics for the reality of the finite world. The Eastern mind laboured equally hard to establish permanently the reality of the Infinite. This difference of attitude explains many other minor characteristics. Modern philosophy insistingly persists in maintaining the permanent importance of preserving the separate identity of our conscious existence. The idea of absorption in the Absolute is a veritable abomination to the Western brain. Personality is conceived to be the highest category known to us; it is therefore the essence of ourselves; and hence our distinct personality must survive in any scheme of ultimate redemption. The Eastern sages consider this stage as a very imperfect one. Personality implies limitation, its limitation by other personalities, and by external environment. Personality implies difference; any union short of identity is more or less external, more or less imperfect. Hence it is incampatible with the idea of an all-round perfection, a complete freedom from limitations. The essence of the personality in fact lies for Hindu philosophers in the soul—the one supreme Self, the Absolute. The essence of the personality is placed by modern psychology in consciousness – in thinking, feeling, and willing. But all that is *manas* according to the *Vedanta*; and *manas* is merely a product of *Maya*. The soul is above all ordinary processes of consciousness, because these as we ordinarily experience them imply many imperfections – such as capacity of growth and decay, capacity of more and less, duality of subject and object, and so on. The soul as perfection, as Reality, must be above all these categories of thinking. But to the Western philosopher, the soul apart from its life in thought, feeling and willing is an abstraction – a mere X, of which we can have no idea whatever.

It is the same with the personality of God. It has no place in the scheme of purely Absolutist metaphysics. Modern Western thought is mostly theistic and its attempt to save differences, to save concreteness in philosophy goes often so far as to make God a finite being, a spatial and temporal God in some systems. In the same way in the eyes of Eastern thinkers, time " is a moving image of eternity " and it,

" Like a dome of many-coloured glass
    Stains the white radiance of eternity."

or as Bergson puts it: " Eternity no longer hovers over time as an abstraction; it underlies time as a reality. "[7] But the Western philosophers do not altogether relish this explaining away of all time and hence we find that an increasing effort is made to conceive time as a part of the essential constitution of Reality. Even the static unity or eternal substance conceived negatively (from the point of view of the world) of the Eastern philosophers has to give way to

---

7. Creative Evolution, p. 335.

a unity dynamically conceived; and even the Absolute is thought of as essentially a growing Absolute. The Bergsonian universe takes the place of the block universe of the ancient thinkers. Change, concreteness, plurality: these are held to be the most vital characteristics of Reality. Perception and its data are more powerful sources of knowledge than conception and its elaborations. The pendulum of thought in the ancient world swung from senses to thought; it has again swung back from thought to senses. Pluralistic theories and pragmatic philosophies typify these tendencies. The ideas of progress, of collective humanity, of morality are asserting their prominence in modern thought and metaphysical systems are so modelled as to explain these facts which are considered fundamental.

Eastern thought has ignored all these matters as of the 'earth, earthy,' and tried to soar above the *here* and *now*, into the timeless, spaceless empyreans of its metaphysical imagination. An individual is an accident, the universe is a freak of *Maya*, time and space are creatures of our brain, causality is a product of our narrow vision, the whole world of facts and thoughts is a mere cosmic illusion, and art and literature, science and philosophy, morality and religion are simple playthings of a baby "who is pleased with a rattle and tickled with a straw or frightened with a bugbear". Like Christ the Eastern sage declares " My kingdom is not of this world." A transcendental view of life and reality, dominates the Eastern thinkers, who try to think as " spectators of all time and existence." The contrast, therefore, is almost complete. It is an eternal fight between changeless and change, between absolute and relative thinking, between the One and the Many, between pure idealism and realism, abstractness and concreteness, between the Infinite and the finite, between complete harmony and identity and differences and discords. Metaphysically the former tendencies are more powerful ; realistically, the latter must decide the situation.

And according as the one or the other tendency predominates, a man leans towards what may be called the Indo-Christian or the Greco-Persian view of life.

We may notice here very briefly a few fundamental points of all Hindu philosophy. (1) Much has been said about the Indian pessimism. All life is conceived as essentially miserable, existence as we understand it ordinarily, is radically evil and fraught with suffering. The essence of this situation is the belief, deep-rooted in oriental thought, that the finite world can never satisfy the infinite spirit of ours. ' यो वै भूमा तत्सुखम् । नाल्पे सुखमस्ति '[8] The belief in the misery of existence is not based upon any hedonistic calculus, upon the excess on the whole of misery over happiness in individual or collective life. The very conditions of life, the limitations of time and space, the change and movement of all existence, make it impossible for our spirit to find final happiness in it. But if worldly existence is fundamentally an evil to

---

8. Ch. 7.23.

be escaped from, that does not mean that the Indian view of life is ultimately dark and pessimistic. As Hegel said "pessimism is the only true basis for optimism." Hindu thought offers to every soul the possibility of emancipation, final and permanent from all finite existence; and this emancipation means a state of boundless, exquisite joy for ever and ever. " यं लब्ध्वा चापरं लाभं मन्यते नाधिकं ततः etc."[9] The Indian view of life is hence ultimately a magnificent optimism. (2) The doctrine of *Karma* that is "the continuous working of every thought, word and deed, through all ages." With this is coupled the (3) doctrine of transmigration. Shankaracharya like other Hindu thinkers, takes it for granted and never makes it a subject of discussion. (4) The belief in the three *gunas* (सत्त्व, रजस्, तमस्) the three constituent elements of nature. *Tamas* is the tendency to passivity, *rajas* is the tendency to activity, and *sattva* is goodness, peace, that passeth understanding. (5) A characteristic feature of

---

9. Bg. 6.22.

all Hindu philosophy is its belief in the infallibility of the *Vedas*. The *Shrutis* were repositories of wisdom acquired by direct experience by the ancient seers. Hence these constituted an authority of no mean weight. (6) The belief in *Moksha* ; as Dr. Deussen says " the belief in liberation is the cornerstone of metaphysics in India."

All Hindu philosophy laboured under one great limitation. The comparative absence of the development of sciences made many portions of our philosophy mere matters of guess-work. The whole modern philosophy stands in this way in broad contrast with all ancient philosophies. Each step in modern philosophy is dictated by a fresh step in science ; and thus philosophy goes on being modelled on the existing scientific knowledge. With the progress of science, there appears a corresponding progress in philosophy. The Hindu philosophy was in this sense largely unprogressive.

This limitation of the scientific knowledge of the ancient Hindus is largely connected with the nature of the Hindu philosophy and its method. Philosophy according to the Hindus was not a sum total of knowledge or wisdom; nor was it a co-ordination of sciences. It was a synoptic view of the whole, a theory of the ultimate reality. Indeed in a sense the view of the office of philosophy among the Hindus curiously coincides to some extent with the view of some of the most modern philosophers of the West. Höffding says that the problem of religion and philosophy alike is the " relation between what seems to us men the highest value and existence as a whole."[10] " We do not so much expect from philosophy " says Windelband " what it was formerly supposed to give, a theoretic scheme of the world, a synthesis of the results of the separate sciences, or transcending them on lines of its own, a scheme harmoniously complete in itself ; what we expect from philosophy to-day is *reflection on those permanent values which have their foundation in a*

---

10. A. S. Pringle-Pattison :"The Idea of God." p. 39.

higher spiritual reality above the changing interests of the times."[11] There is indeed much difference in the view about the values which may be considered of ultimate validity, but the task of Hindu philosophy may be said to be fundamentally the same. It is investigation into the highest Reality, and the values which may be conserved in the highest Reality.

The method of Hindu philosophy is generally the high *a priori* method by which we proceed from the whole to the parts, and not the empirical one of rising from the parts to the whole. The reality of the whole, the unity and eternity of the Absolute and such other beliefs are taken for granted and all subsequent inquiry is into the relations of the finite and the Infinite and so on. But we may say that this was generally the method of the Greek philosophy and also of many great speculative systems of the modern period. This deductive, *a priori*, dogmatic method is not quite palatable to

---

11. ibid. p. 39.

the modern scientific brain, but it is often eminently suited to philosophy, and often the only one possible in the science of the Absolute.

This is the method of Shankaracharya. Many criticisms are levelled against such a procedure. The Absolute is said to be " shot out of a pistol " in a system like this. Experience is neglected and reality is explained by *a priori* notions. Unity which philosophy seeks should be not the *prius* of all inquiry, its first assumption, but rather it is the end to be ultimately attained, the last goal of all speculation. It should not be merely postulated at the outset as Shankara does, but demonstrated to be the possible ideal towards which all knowledge and being are moving. Otherwise, philosophy may be charged with being dogmatic and hence not entitled to the attention of scientific people. Further, it is argued by Ward that, " The first essential of philosophy is organic coherence; it cannot, so to say have two independent growing points ; and so long as experience is the one there cannot be any finality about philosophy......On experience as it develops the idea of the pure reason may rise to perish never ; but it was certainly not discernible at first ; and if present now, its full meaning is ineffable still."[12]

This criticism is not quite fair. The method of metaphysics is not the same as the method of science. But none the less it is an appropriate method for philosophy. Philosophy does not ignore experience. It is our ordinary commonsense view of things which comes first; and when we find on deeper reflection that it is partial and inadequate, we are led to more fundamental views about the universe. Experience, is therefore, the starting-point of Shankara's system as well as that of other systems. In fact, it is the only possible starting-point for all people, philosophers as well as non-philosophers. Edward Caird says : " Metaphysics does not proceed to create the world out of its own categories, still less to supersede the special work of

---

12. Ward : The Realm of Ends. : p. 22-3.

science. On the contrary, it is through the discovery of the partial and inadequate explanation of things which the categories of science furnish that it is led to seek after a deeper satisfaction for thought, an interpretation of the world by higher principles, till it attains that final interpretation which is given by a principle which rests on none higher, but is seen by its own light. Reversing the process, it then seeks to show how all the previous stages of knowledge from the highest to the lowest, become transformed in the light of the first principle of knowledge, or how all things are seen in their reality only when regarded as its expressions or manifestations."[13]

---

13. Caird : Spinoza. p. 132-3.

CHAPTER II

SHANKARA'S ATTITUDE TOWARDS OTHER OPPOSED SYSTEMS

We shall give, in brief, Shankara's refutation of the various rival views. This work occupies a large amount of space in his writings. Shankara himself gives a justification of this polemic in his work: " An opponent might come forward and say that we are indeed entitled to establish our own position, so as to define perfect knowledge which is the means of release to those desirous of it, but that no use is apparent of a refutation of other opinions, a proceeding productive of nothing but hate and anger. There is a use, we reply. For there is some danger of men of inferior intelligence looking upon the *Samkhya* and similar systems as requisite for perfect knowledge, because these systems have a weighty appearance, have been adopted by authoritative persons and profess to lead to perfect knowledge." [1] And further, we are able to get a more critical knowledge of his own system by the contrast he himself draws between his own thought and that of others.

Refutation of the Samkhyas. [2] The Samkhyas maintain that the non-intelligent *pradhana* consisting of three elements, is the cause of the world. The *Vedanta* passages can be construed to support this position. The *pradhana* is omnipotent; because it has all the effects for its objects. It is omniscient, because knowledge is an attribute of goodness (सत्व), one of its constituents. And omniscience means capacity for all knowledge for the *Brahman* as well as *pradhana*; because otherwise (if it means active cognition of everything) if cognition were permanent, the *Brahman* would be dependent upon the activity of knowing; if

---
1. S. B. II. 2. 1.
2. S. B. (I. i. 5-11), (I. 4. 1-13), (I. 4. 28) (II. I. 1-2). (II. 2. 1-10.)

it were non-permanent, the *Brahman* would cease along with it. Moreover, previously to the Creation, the *Brahman* is without any instruments of action or knowledge. And further, the *pradhana*, as consisting of various elements, is capable of undergoing modifications and may therefore act as a (material) cause like clay; while the uncompounded homogenous *Brahman* is unable to do so.

The refutation is as follows. This view is unscriptural: the *shrutis* ascribe intelligence to the first cause. " स ईक्षां चक्रे " etc. The *pradhana*, again, has no more right to be called all-knowing, because of the presence of the *sattva guna* in it, than little-knowing, because of the presence of the *rajas* and *tamas gunas*. Further, an act of knowledge always requires a witnessing principle, but the *pradhana* is non-intelligent. Again, the cognitional activity of the *Brahman* must be permanent. Like the sun, whose light and heat are permanent and which is still independent of any reference to outward object (when we say the sun shines), the *Brahman* also may be spoken of as an agent without reference to any object of knowledge. Still, if it be said that an object of thought is necessary for thought, the *Brahman* can think of names and forms which are involved, before the Creation. Nor does the *Brahman* stand in any need of any organs or instruments. And there is a consensus of the *Vedanta* authorities in favour of the view that the intelligent *Brahman* is the cause of the world.

In the second part of the second Book of the Brahma-Sutras, an independent refutation is attempted. The *Samkhyas* argue as follows :— Just as jars, dishes and other products which possess the common quality of consisting of clay are seen to have for their cause clay in general, so we must suppose that all the inanimate and animate objects are endowed with the characteristics of pleasure, pain and dullness in general. Pleasure, pain and dullness in their generality together constitute the threefold *pradhana*. This non-intelligent *pradhana* evolves itself spontaneously into multiform modifications in order thus to effect the purposes of the intelligent soul.

Now if the *Samkhya* theory is thus based on observation merely, Shankara rejoins on the basis of observation that such a wonderful organization as the universe requires an intelligent and not a non-intelligent cause. Clay itself does not shape itself into pots etc, it requires potters to mould it into the jars and dishes. Again, the presence of activity in the world requires an intelligent agent. Chariots indeed move, but that is due to the intelligent driver. Activity indeed belongs to non-intelligent things, but it results from an intelligent principle. True, the nature of the soul is pure intelligence, still it can move the universe although itself unmoving, (as a magnet moves iron). The pure *Brahman* does not move, but motion is still explained intelligently within the empirical sphere.

If the *pradhana* works spontaneously, it has no reference to a purpose. If purpose were admitted, it would be either enjoyment or release. But the soul (आत्मा) is by its very nature incapable of any accretion of pleasure or pain ; and it is in a state of perpetual release. Neither the *pradhana* nor the pure soul can feel any desire. It is said that the soul like a lame man guiding the *pradhana*, a blind man, or that the soul moves the *pradhana*, as the magnet moves iron. But this would contradict the previous position, according to which the *pradhana* is moving of itself and the inactive soul possesses no moving power. If the soul moves the *pradhana* by means of proximity, permanency of motion would follow from the permanency of proximity ; and the possibility of final release will be cut off.

Refutation of the Atomists (वैशेषिक).[3] The *Vaisheshiks* maintain that the universe originates from atoms, through the operation of an unseen principle. But how did motion take place at all ? Neither endeavour nor impact is possible at the time of the original

---

3. S. B. (11. 2. 12-17)

motion. The unseen principle also cannot explain the phenomenon. An unintelligent principle cannot of itself act or be the cause of action. (Vide the refutation of the *Samkhyas*). If the unseen principle is supposed to inhere in the soul to be connected with the atoms, then there would result continuity of action (because soul is all-pervading). Thus there is no original cause of action; original action cannot take place in the atoms.

The notion of conjunction of atoms also presents difficulties. Conjunction takes place only between substances having parts. The essential activity or non-activity of the atoms themselves also does not take us further. For on the former hypothesis, *pralaya* (destruction) is impossible; on the latter belief, the Creation is unaccountable.

The arguments advanced to establish the permanency of atoms are not valid. The first argument is that the atoms have no cause; hence they are permanent. But the atoms possess the qualities of colour etc ; and they are therefore gross and non-permanent, compared to their ultimate cause. The second argument is that the special negation implied in the word non-eternal implies that there is an eternal thing. Well, that eternal thing may not be an atom, but may be the *Brahman*. And we cannot argue from words to things. The third argument is that the impossibility of conceiving a third reason of the destruction of effects, in addition to the division of the causal substance into its parts and the destruction of the causal substance, involves the permanency of the atoms. This is correct, if a new substance is produced only by the conjunction of several causal substances. But a causal substance may originate a new substance by passing over into a qualified state, and the effected object may be destroyed by the dissolution of its inner relations.

Further, if the atoms have the same qualities as the elements, whose causes they are, some will have greater number of qualities than others and hence greater size than other atoms. If all atoms have one quality only, the elements must have one quality also. Or if all the atoms have all the four qualities, then water must have smell, air must have taste, colour, smell and so on.

The *Vaisheshiks* maintain that their six categories are absolutely different from each other and yet assume that they depend upon substance. This account is contradictory. Again, if the qualities etc. depend upon substance, substance alone exists. Smoke indeed is different from fire and yet dependent upon it. But smoke and fire are apperceived.

The relation of conjunction is not possible between the soul and the internal organ and the atoms, because these do not consist of parts. The *Samaraya* (inherence) relation alone is possible between that which abides and that which forms the abode. But this would involve the vice of mutual dependence, for only when the separateness of cause and effect is established, the relation of the abode and that which abides can be established;

and only when the latter relation is established, the reason of separateness can be proved.

It thus appears that the atomic doctrine is supported by weak arguments, it is opposed to scriptural passages and it is not accepted by any of the authorities taking their stand on scripture, such as Manu and the others.

Refutation of the Realist (सर्वास्तित्ववादिन्) *Bauddhas* :— The Bauddhas of realistic tendencies maintain that everything external as well as internal, is real. What is external is element or elemental (भौतिक) ; what is internal is mind (चित्त) or mental (चैत). The elements are earth, water etc ; elemental are colour etc, on the one hand, and the eye and the other sense-organs on the other hand. The inward world consists of five groups-sensation, feeling, knowledge, verbal knowledge, impressions.

Now how these two classes of aggregates (material and skandhas) (bodies and minds) can be brought about is not clear. The

---
4. S. B. (II. 2. 18-27).

Bauddhas do not believe in any permanent intelligent being, soul or God. If they move themselves, they will never cease to be active. Nor can the cause lie in the train of self-cognitions (आलयविज्ञानप्रवाह); for if this train is different from a single self-cognition, it is permanent and then it is nothing else but the soul of the *Vedantin*; and if it is the same as a single self-cognition, it is momentary and hence without influence. Nescience cannot account for their existence, because it presupposes their existence. And an eternal chain of aggregates means that aggregates produce their own like or unlike aggregates. If the former is true, man cannot be a god or an animal (cannot transmigrate in the next life into these existences); in the latter case, man might in an instant be turned into an elephant or a god. Further, as there is no permanent Self, no being desirous of release can be assumed.

The doctrine of momentariness renders causality an impossibility. We may say A is; B is. But to say that B follows A, would mean connection between the two ; but A perishes in the first moment and has nothing to do with B. If it is said that an effect may arise in the absence of a cause, then anything might originate from anything.

The fact of remembrance also refutes the doctrine of universal momentariness for remembrance implies the continuity of the person. Nor will it do to say that the recognition takes place owing to the similarity of the different self-cognitions ; for the cognition of similarity is based on two things. The judgment of similarity cannot be quite a new act ; the expression, ' this is similar to that ', contradicts it. We alway feel that we are conscious of it being that. Doubts may arise as regards the identity of similarity of outward things ; but no doubts are possible regarding the continuity of the person, of the conscious subject.

The absence of permanent, stable causes leads to the belief that entity can spring from non-entity. But such a position is entirely unacceptable. It would run counter to our normal experience in which we see special causes producing special effects. If undifferentiated non-existence has causal efficiency, all things will emanate from all things. But such is not the case. If the theory of the *Bauddhas* were true, rice would grow for the husbandman, if he did not cultivate his field ; vessels would shape themselves, even if the potter did not fashion the clay and so on. No effort would be necessary for any object whatsoever.

Refutation of the Subjective Idealists (विज्ञानैकस्कंधवादिन्.)[5] These philosophers maintain that external things do not exist, they must be either atoms or aggregates of atoms. But such minute things as atoms cannot be apprehended ; and aggregates of atoms cannot be thought of as different from atoms, nor as identical with them (not different because they are composed of atoms nor identical for they would not be then observed in all their parts). What exists is therefore the

---
5. S. B. (II, 2. 28-32.)

mental process of knowledge connected with the mind. Further, ideas have the same form as the object; that is the form of the object is determined by the ideas. Hence these are identical. Again, we are simultaneously conscious of the fact of knowledge and the object of knowledge; this also proves the identity of the idea and the object. Perception is similar to a dream. The variety of ideas is due to the impressions left by the previous ideas. In the beginningless *Samsara* ideas and impressions succeed each other as causes and effects.

The *Vedantin* replies that this reasoning is not correct. External things exist, because we are conscious of them. Nobody when perceiving a post or a wall, is conscious of his perception only, but all men are conscious of posts, walls, and the like as objects of their perceptions. All the instruments of knowledge (प्रमाणः) testify to the truth of this consciousness. Again, if there were no objects, ideas cannot have the same form as the objects, and objects are actually apprehended as external. Things and ideas are perceived simultaneously because they are related as cause and effect, not because they are identical.

To say that ideas are self-luminous while external things are not so, is not reasonable. The idea is apprehended only as belonging to a Self, and existence of Self is self-proved. This Self is quite distinct from the ideas (of the *Bauddhas*) ; the latter originate, pass away, are manifold ; while the Self is one and permanent.

It is idle to say that our ideas are like dreams. The latter are negated by the consciousness of our waking state ; the former are not ; the latter are the results of remembrance : while the ideas of the active state are acts of immediate consciousness. The results of the ingenious sophistries of the so-called philosophers cannot wipe out our belief in the data of our immediate consciousness. The fact that the dreams and ideas of the waking state have some attributes in common does not mean anything. Fire has certain attributes in common with water; but it does not follow that it is cold.

Further, the variety of mental impressions is caused altogether by the variety of things perceived: hence the *Bauddhas* cannot account for them. All impressions require a substratum which the *Bauddhas* do not admit, because it cannot be cognised. The self-cognition (आलयविज्ञान) cannot be the abode of the mental impressions; because it is momentary.

The *Shunya Vada* (or nihilism) does not need special refutation. The apparent world, whose existence is guaranteed by all the means of right knowledge, cannot be denied, unless some one should find out some new truth on the basis of which he may impugn its existence.

Refutation of the Jainas :—[6] The Jainas apply the following reasoning to all things :— somehow it is, somehow it is not: somehow it is and it is not: somehow it is and is indescribable; somehow it is not and

---

6. S. B. II. 2. 33-36.

is indescribable; somehow it is and it is not and is indescribable. Well, such a doctrine of relativity is nothing but a bundle of contradictions. Such contradictory attributes as being and non-being cannot belong at one and the same time to one and the same thing; just as observation teaches us that a thing cannot be hot and cold at the same time. The whole reasoning is very unsettling: the result is vagueness and confusion. No definite assertion is possible; and we are landed in agnosticism or scepticism. Further it is impossible to act upon such theories; because of their contradictory and chaotic nature. Hence the practical teaching of the *Jainas* about bondage and release will be of no avail.

The *Jainas* maintain that the soul has the same size as the body. This makes the soul limited and perishable. Further, the same soul cannot accommodate itself to bodies of varying sizes. It may be said that the infinite particles of souls are capable of compression and dilation. Well, then, if particles cannot occupy the same space, it follows that an infinite number of particles cannot be contained in a limited body. If they can occupy the same position, the soul will be of minute size. The hypothesis of the successive accession and withdrawal of particles is also not tenable. It would mean that the soul is changable, and hence non-eternal. Hence this view will contradict the *Jainas'* views about final release. Again, these particles are either material or non-material. In the former case they cannot be distinguished from body; in the latter case there must be a reservoir of soul-particles whence they come. But we do not know of any such reservoir. Lastly the *Jainas* believe in the permanency of the final size of the soul; from this would follow that the size in previous conditions is also permanent.

Refutation of the Pashupatas :— 7 The main position to be rebutted here is that the Lord is merely the operative cause of the world and not the material cause. In that

---

7. S. B. II. 2. 37-41.

case God will be responsible for the inequalities in the world. Secondly, all activity argues some imperfection in the agent. Thirdly, the Lord cannot be active on this theory, because he is represented as a special kind of soul. Fourthly, no reasonable connection can be established on this hypothesis between God, and the souls. Fifthly, the Lord, like the ruler of a country must have a body; but previous to the Creation there are no bodies. And still if we suppose a material substratum for him, he will be subject to the sensations of ordinary transmigratory souls and will cease to be the Lord. Sixthly, the Lord either defines the measure of the *pradhana*, the souls and himself, or not. If the former all these will have an end, and consequently a beginning. This will lead us to the doctrine of a general void. And if the measure of the Lord himself, the *pradhana*, and the souls is not defined by the Lord, he is not omniscient.

Refutation of the Bhagvatas :— [8] The

---

8. S. B. II 2. 42-45. 9. S. B. III. 3. 54-55.

Bhagvatas are of opinion that Vasudeva whose nature is pure knowledge divides himself four-fold : Vasudeva, the highest Self ; Sankarshana, the individual soul ; Pradumna the mind, and Aniruddha, the principle of egoity. Vasudeva is the causal essence ; the three others are an effect, otherwise he will be non-permanent. Release will become impossible ; for the effect is absorbed only by entering into its cause. Further, an instrument such as a hatchet is never observed to spring from an agent such as Devadatta. But the Bhagvatas teach that mind springs from the individual soul.

If it is said that all these four are equally perfect Lords, then we rejoin that there is no necessity of assuming four ultimate causes, when one is sufficient. Again from the one Vasudeva cannot spring equally powerful beings. A cause must have some superiority over the effect. In fact, all the world is a manifestation of one Vasudeva. The doctrine is also full of contradictions.

Refutation of the Materialists :— The

materialists see the Self in the body and deny the existence of a Self apart from the body. Consciousness (चैतन्य) springs from external elements, in the form of intellect, just as the power of intoxication (from fermenting matter). The body alone, therefore, is the conscious being ; and the Self, because a conscious being only continues as long as the body, a separate abode is not proved ; hence the Self cannot persist beyond the body.

But this is not true ; the existence of the Self is not dependent upon the existence of the body. The very argument of the materialists can be turned against them. The materrialists argue that the qualities of the Self are qualities of the body, because they persist as long as the body. We may rejoin that the qualities of the Self are not the qualities of the body, because they do not persist while the body persists. Shape etc. persist, but motion, remembrance etc. do not persist in the state of death. Further, while the former are perceived by others, the latter are not perceived. The qualities of the

Self may persist by entering into another body.

Form and colour and other qualities (of the elements) do not make their own form or colour or the form and colour of something else their objects. But consciousness can render elements and their products its objects ; hence it cannot be a quality of any body. Because consciousness makes the material world known (and not *vice versa*) consciousness must be separate from the latter. This consciousness constitutes the nature of the Self. And we may infer from the fact of the identity of the conscious agent in such mental acts as recollection that consciousness is one. From the unity of consciousness therefore we may argue the unity of the Self and its independence of the body and its consequent eternity.

Moreover, perceptive consciousness takes place where there are certain auxiliaries such as lamps and the like, and does not arise from their absence. Still it is not an attribute of lamp or the like. In the same way, the body is used by the Self as an auxiliary. Further, in the state of dream, we have perceptions, while the body is motionless. Hence the Self is separate from the body.

CHAPTER III

METAPHYSICS

Brahman or the Absolute has a twofold appearance in the *Vedanta* system. It is now described in terms of phenomena, now it is mentioned as a pure noumenon. "*Brahman* is apprehended under two forms; in the first place as qualified by limiting conditions owing to the multiformity of the evolutions of name and form; in the second place as being the opposite of this i. e. free from all limiting conditions whatever."[1] The reason for this distinction is to be sought in the different levels of culture of the persons addressing themselves to God. " Although one and the same Self is hidden in all beings movable as well as immovable, yet owing to the gradual rise of excellence of the minds which form the limiting conditions (of the Self) (उपाधिविशेषतारतम्यात्), Scripture declares that the Self,* although eternally unchanging and uniform, reveals itself in a graduated series of beings, and so appears in forms of various dignity and power."[2] The *Shastras* therefore lay down all instructions as regards the goal to be attained and the special means to be adopted for it with special reference to the varieties of temperaments and talents among men.[3]

Metaphysics is concerned mainly with the undifferentiated *Brahman*, the pure Absolute. It is mainly described in a negative way, by a reference to what it is not than what it is. It is frequently said that it is above speech and thought.[4] " It stands to reason that *Brahman* cannot be expressed in words such as *Sat* and *Asat* (existing and non-existing); for every word employed to denote a thing denotes that thing – when

---

* Leibniz's conception of monads–each one realising Reality from its own point of view with more or less distinctness–is a parallel.

1. S. B. I. 2. 14.   2. S. B. I. 1. 11.
3. Br. C. II 1. 20.   4. Br. C. II. 3. 1.

heard by another — as associated with a certain *genus* or a certain *act*, or a certain *quality*, or a certain mode of relation...But *Brahman* belongs to no genus...It possesses no qualities...It is actionless ... It is not related to anything else...Hence it is but right to say that it can be denoted by no word at all."⁵ It is therefore described as neither being (सत्) nor non-being (असत्). Shankara explains this by saying that it is neither the object of consciousness of existence, nor of non-existence, because it is beyond the reach of the senses.⁶ It must not be understood by this negative way of expressing the nature of *Brahman* that it is a mere abstraction or negation. Nothing can be more remote from truth. " After the clause ' not so, not so ' has given information about *Brahman* the clause next following illustrates this teaching by saying : There is nothing beyond nor separate from *Brahman* therefore *Brahman* is expressed by ' not so,

---

5. Bg. C. XIII. 12. Br. C. II. 3. 6.
6 Bg. C. XIII. 2.

METAPHYSICS

not so' which latter words do not mean that *Brahman* itself does not exist. The implied meaning rather is that different from everything else, there exists the 'non-negatived' *Brahman*."[7]

The pure *Brahman* has, however, some positive characteristics ascribed to it. The first general fact about it is its existence. Here, however, we must discriminate. Existence as we understand it ordinarily is either an idea or a physical fact. Such attributes as existence, non-existence are derived from our notions of change, absence of change, combination of both or absolute negation. These attributes therefore far from expressing the nature of Reality only serve to delude us.[8] In the commentary on the *Gita*, an opponent says everything must be comprised under one of the two categories existence or non-existence. Shankara replies that this is correct as regards objects of sense-perception. But *Brahman* being supersensible (अतीन्द्रिय) need not be an object of consciousness of

---
7. S. B. III. 2. 22.   8. Karikas IV. 83.

existence or non-existence.⁹ But because empirical existence does not belong to *Brahman*, we cannot deny of it all existence. On the other hand, *Brahman* alone exists; it is the same thing as Existence; outside it or different from it there is no existence. It is defined as Existence.¹⁰ It is described as (वस्तासामान्य)¹¹ (existence in general).

The second characteristic which also forms the very nature of pure *Brahman*, is its Intelligence. It is described variously as चित्, चैतन्य, etc. ¹² " Intelligence is its very nature as heat and light constitute the very nature of heat." The following discussion in the हस्तामलकीयभाष्य throws much light on this aspect of *Brahman*. It is, different from ordinary knowledge or intelligence; because the latter is the effect and hence liable to be stultified by an opposite impression; hence it is not eternal. But *Brahman* is eternal, and hence it is चैतन्य not ज्ञान. All ज्ञान, or knowledge is an object of

---

9. Bg. C. XIII. 12.　　10. S. B. II. 1. 6.
11. T. C. Br. valli. I.　　12. S. B. II. 3. 13.

knowledge ; hence it is unintelligent (जड). Whatever is an object of experience cannot be a subject ; hence ordinary knowledge cannot belong to the essence of *Brahman*. What then is the proof of this ? Everybody knows that the world is an object of insight. What is the source of this illumination ? Not ordinary knowledge ; because it is itself unintelligent. Hence it is established that it is known through the light of the Self. Now the question arises whether *Brahman* (or the Self) stands in the relation of a substance and an attribute to intelligence ? In that case intelligence must be either different from, the same as or both different and non-different from *Brahman*. The last case is not possible, because it involves us in a contradiction. Nor does the first alternative hold good. Because the relation of conjunction is not possible ; because intelligence is not a substance ; and the relation of inherence (समवाय) involves a *regressus ad infinitum*. And if they are not the same, there is no possibility of the relation of a quality and a substance between the Self and Intelligence. Whiteness cannot be the quality of whiteness. Hence the Self does not possess the attribute of intelligence (चिद्धर्म); but its very nature is intelligence (चित्स्वरूप). In the same way we can reason as to the other attributes of pure *Brahman*, viz. existence and joy.[13] The same truth is expressed in the commentary on the *sutras*. " The Self has neither inside nor outside any characteristic form but intelligence; simple non-differentiated intelligence constituted its nature; just as a lump of salt has inside as well as outside one and the same saltish taste, not any other taste." [14] " The question arises whether *Brahman* is to be defined as that which is (सत्) or as thought, or as both...How can *Brahman*, if devoid of intelligence, be said to be the Self of the intelligent individual soul? And how could we admit thought apart from existence? Nor can it be said that *Brahman* has both these characteristics, since that would con-

---

13. H. C. 2. also see T. Br. vall. C, I.
14. S. B. III, 2, 16.

tradict something already admitted. For he who would maintain that *Brahman* is characterised by thought different from existence, and at the same time by existence different from thought, would virtually maintain that there is a plurality in *Brahman*. — But as scripture teaches both (viz. that *Brahman* is one only and that it possesses more than one characteristic) there can be no objection to such a doctrine. There is we reply, for one being cannot possibly possess more than one nature. And if finally, it should be said that existence is thought and thought existence and that the two do not exclude each other ; we remark that in that case there is no reason for doubt whether *Brahman* is that which is or intelligence or both." [15]

Shankara did not quite clearly express himself whether esoteric *Brahman* is of the nature of joy (आनंद) also. In I. 1. 19. he says that it forms a part of the definition of the qualified *Brahman*. " If by the Self

---

15. S. B. III. 2. 21,

consisting of bliss we were to understand *Brahman*, we should have to assume that the *Brahman* meant is the *Brahman* distinguished by qualities (सगुण)...Moreover as joy etc. differ in each individual body, *Brahman*, on the other hand, does not differ according to bodies."[16] In the next passage he says " Other attributes, however, such as bliss and so on which scripture sets forth for the purpose of teaching the true nature of *Brahman* are to be viewed as valid for all passages referring to *Brahman*; for their purport i. e. *Brahman* whose nature is to be taught, is one. Those attributes are mentioned with a view to knowledge only, not to meditation."[17]

Now we will describe the other aspects of *Brahman* which is known as सगुण or सविशेष or सोपाधिक ब्रह्म (the differentiated *Brahman*.) This *Brahman* is the same as the God (ईश्वर) of our theology. " The Lord depends (as Lord) upon the limiting adjuncts of names and forms, the products of nescience ; just as

---

16. S. B. I. 1. 19.   17. S. B. III. 3. 13.

the universal ether depends (as limited ether, such as the ether of a jar etc.) upon the limiting adjuncts in the shape of jars, pots, &c. He (the Lord) stands in the realm of the phenomenal in the relation of a ruler to the so-called *jivas* (individual souls) or cognitional selves (विज्ञानात्मन्) which indeed are one with his own Self."[18]

This *Brahman* is defined as:— " That omniscient, omnipotent cause from which proceed the origin, subsistence, and dissolution of this world-which world is differentiated by names and forms, contains many agents and enjoyers, is the abode of the fruits of actions, these fruits having their definite places, times, and causes, and the nature of whose arrangements cannot be even conceived by the mind-that cause, we say, is *Brahman*."[19] *Brahman* which is all-knowing and endowed with all powers whose essential nature is eternal purity, intelligence and freedom, exists. For, if we consider, the derivation of the word ' *Brahman* ' from

---

18. S. B. II. 1. 14.   19. S. B. I. 1. 2.

the root '*brih*' 'to be great' we at once understand that eternal purity, and so on belong to *Brahman*.'[20]

The justification of conceiving a differentiated *Brahman* lies in the needs of our religious nature. Popular religious consciousness requires for the purposes of worship the existence of God (or a personal God). The qualified *Brahman* is the personal God of Christian, Hindu and other theisms. Personality is not attributed to the Absolute, because it is more than personal. Personality in fact, is, too low a determination of *Brahman*. Our ordinary conception of personality requires an outward environment upon which it acts and in conflict or co-operation with which it develops itself. But if we broaden our idea of personality, if we mean by it a unity of consciousness, a centre of intelligence which completely possesses itself and fully controls all its activities, we may say with Lotze that true personality is with the Infinite. The Absolute, therefore, is,

---
20. S. B, I, 1. 1.

super-personal, as it is super-moral and super-rational. The idea of God in the *Vedanta*, however, fully meets all our theistic requirements of a personal God. " As long as *Brahman* is the object of nescience there are applied to it the categories of devotee, object of devotion, and the like. The different modes of devotion lead to different results, some to exaltation, some to gradual emancipation, some to success in the works; these modes are distinct on account of the distinction of the different qualities and limiting conditions."[21] In this way the most abstract and highly impersonal theories of the Absolute give way not only to a personal God but to other forms of worship as well, for the purposes of the less advanced people.

Shankara in his esoteric metaphysics maintains that the pure *Brahman* cannot be demonstrated. But it is possible to infer the existence of God from certain empirical facts. The first proof is psychological " The exist-

---

21, S. B. I, 1, 11.

ence of *Brahman* is demonstrated by the fact that it is the Self of all. For everyone assumes the existence of himself, for he cannot say, " I am not ". For if the existence of the Self were not demonstrated, then all the world could say ' I am not '. And the Self is *Brahman* ".[22] The second is epistemological proof. " Because the Self is the basis of the action of proving, and consequently it is evident before the action of proving. And since it is of this character it is therefore impossible to deny it. " The third proof is teleological. (a) Presence of order in the world argues the presence of intelligence in its authorship. " Look at this entire world which appears, on the one hand as external (i. e. inanimate) in the form of earth and the other elements enabling (the souls) to enjoy the fruits of their various actions, and on the other hand, as animate in the form of bodies which belong to the different classes of beings, possess a definite arrangement of organs, and are therefore

---
22. S. B. I. 1. 1.

capable of constituting the abodes of fruition; look we say at this world of which even the most ingenious workman cannot form a conception in the mind, and then say if a non-intelligent principle is able to fashion it." [23] (b) Activity also means the work of intelligence. It indeed belongs to non-intelligent things in which it is observed, but " it results from an intelligent principle, because it exists when the latter is present and does not exist when the latter is absent." Pure intelligence is itself devoid of motion; but it may nevertheless move other things. [24] The fourth proof is cosmological. "*Brahman* which is mere Being cannot spring from mere being, since the relation of cause and effect cannot exist without a relation of superiority (on the part of the cause). Nor again can *Brahman* spring from that which is something particular, since this would be contrary to experience. For we observe that particular forms of experience are produced from what is general, as for instance, jars and pots from

---

23. S. B. II. 2. 2. 1.   24. S. B. II. 2. 2.

clay, but not what is general is produced from particulars. Nor again can *Brahman* spring from that which is not (*asat*) for that which is not is without a self...Further, the non-admission of a fundamental causal substance would drive us to a *retrogressus in infinitum*."[25]

God is above time, above space, and above causality. Infinity belongs to the very essence of His nature. *Atman* is eternal (नित्य); because it has existence and it has no cause, just like an atom. *Atman* exists, because every-body feels that 'I exist'. It has no cause; its cause is not perceived by ordinary *pramanas* (means of knowledge); nor is it laid down in the *shrutis*; and because it is stated to be the cause of all the three worlds in the *shrutis*.[26] "*Brahman* is infinite in three respects—in respect of time, in respect of space and in respect of things respectively. *Akasha* for example, is infinite in space. But *Akasha* is not infinite either in respect of time or in respect of things. Why?—Because

---

25. S. B. II. 3. 9.   26. H. C. 2.

it is an effect. Unlike *Akasha*, *Brahman* is unlimited even in respect of time, because it is not an effect. What forms an effect is alone limited by time...so, too, in respect of things.—How is it infinite in respect of things?—Because it is inseparable from all. That thing indeed which is separate from another, forms the limits of that other; for when the mind is engaged in the former, it is withdrawn from the latter. There is no such separation in the case of *Brahman*. He is therefore unlimited in respect of things. Here one may ask: How is *Brahman* inseparable from all? Listen, Because it is the cause of all things, time, *Akasha* and so on. Then *Brahman* is limited by other things, and so far as there are other things called effects. (Answer) No because the things spoken of effects are unreal. Apart from the cause, there is indeed no such thing as an effect really existing at which the idea of the cause may terminate; and *shruti* says: (All) changing form (विकार) is a name, a creation of speech. So in the first place, as the cause of *Akasha* etc. *Brahman* is infinite in space; for it is admitted by all that *Akasha* is unlimited space. And *Brahman* is the cause of *Akasha*...Indeed an all-pervading thing is never found to arise from that which is not all-pervading. Hence the *Atman's* absolute infinitude as concerns space. Similarly not being an effect, *Atman* is infinite as concerns time, and owing to absence of anything separate from it, it is infinite in respect of things. Hence its absolute reality."[27]

Brahman is defined as " that from which proceed the origination, sustention and retractation of the world."[28] It is therefore both the material and efficient cause, because that from which some other thing springs and into which it returns is well-known to be the material cause of that other thing. It is the operative cause because there is no other ruling principle and because of its intelligence.[29] This view is open to certain objections. First, the world as an effect is differ-

---

27. T. C. Br. vall. I.   28. S. B. I. 1. 2.
29. S. B. I. 4, 23-27.

ent from *Brahman* its cause.[30] To this objection it is replied that (a) from man who is acknowledged to be intelligent, non-intelligent things such as hair, nail, originate. (b) if absolute equality were insisted on (in case of one thing being the effect of another) the relation of material cause and effect (which after all requires a distinction between the two) would be annihilated.

2. If *Brahman* is the cause of non-intelligent world, it follows that the effect has to be considered as non-existing before its actual origination. But the consequence cannot be acceptable to the *Vedantin* who maintains that the effect exists in the cause already. This objection is not valid. In so far as the effect exists through its participation in the nature of the cause, its existence is the same before the actual beginning of the effect. (as after it.)[31]

3. The effect inquinates the cause with its properties at the time of re-absorption. No. Things for instance, made of clay, such

---

30. S. B. II. 1. 5.   31. S. B. II. 1. 7.

as pots etc., which in this state of separate existence are of various descriptions, do not when they are re-absorped into their original matter (i. e.) clay, impart to the latter their individual qualities. And as the magician is not affected at any time by the magical illusion produced by himself, because it is unreal, so the highest Self is not affected by the world-illusion.[32]

4. If we assume all distinctions to pass (at the time of re-absorption) into the state of non-distinction, there would be no special reason for the origin of a new world affected with distinctions. This objection is also refuted by the parallel instances of deep sleep and trance.[33]

5. The doctrine of *Brahman's* causality must be abandoned, as it leads to the sublation of the well-established distinction of enjoyers and the objects of enjoyment. To this it is replied that " It may exist as in ordinary experience. We see, for instance, that waves, foam, bubbles, and other modi-

---

[32]. S. B. II. 1. 9.   [33]. S. B. II. 1. 9.

fications of the sea, although they really are not different from the sea-water, exist, sometimes in the state of mutual separation, sometimes in the state of conjunction."[34]

6. If the doctrine is accepted, certain faults, as for instance, doing what is not beneficial, will attach (to the intelligent cause i. e. *Brahman*). No, these faults adhere to the embodied self. *Brahman* is eternally free ; there is nothing beneficial to be done by it, nor non-beneficial to be avoided by it.[35]

7. How can *Brahman* act as a Creator without providing itself with instruments to work with ? The absolutely complete power of *Brahman* does not require to be supplemented by any extraneous help.[36]

8. *Brahman* which is not composed of parts cannot undergo the change into its effects. As partial modification is impossible, a modification of the entire *Brahman* has to be assumed. But that involves a cutting off

---

34. S. B. II. 1. 13.   35. S. B. II. 1 22-23.
36. S. B. II. 1. 24-25.

of *Brahman* from its very basis. Shankara refutes these objections by the evidence of *Shruti*. But the opponent says that the holy texts cannot make us understand what is contradictory. If *Brahman* is without parts, it does not undergo a change at all, or it changes in its entirety. Shankara says that change is due to illusion only.[37]

9. *Brahman* cannot act without organs. It is replied that *Brahman* possesses all possible capacities.

10. If the Creation serves some purpose of the intelligent highest Self, its self-sufficiency is destroyed; if you assume absence of motive on its part, you must assume absence of activity also. And if we assume it to act like a mad man, its omniscience is affected.—We reply, the activity of the Lord may be supposed to be a mere sport, proceeding from His own nature, without reference to any purpose.[38]

11. The Lord cannot be the cause of the world because on that hypothesis, the re-

---

37. S. B. II. 1. 26. 27.   38. S. B. II. 1. 32.—33.

proach of inequality of dispensation and cruelty would attach to him—But the Lord is bound by regards; he has to look to merit and demerit. As the *Samsara* is without beginning, merit and inequality are like seed and sprout, caused as well as causes.[39]

Now if *Brahman* is the creator of the whole world, is it the creator of the individual souls also ? No, the soul is the unmodified *Brahman*; it cannot be a product. It is not in itself divided; it only appears divided owing to its limiting adjuncts.[40]

Some regard the soul to be of atomic size. But it is not of atomic size. It is identical with *Brahman*, and as *Brahman* is all-pervading or infinite the soul is infinite likewise. All statements contradicting this fundamental fact about the soul are due to *Avidya* (nescience).[41]

The intelligence of the soul is adventitious according to Kanada and others; it is produced by the conjunction of the self with the

---

39. S. B. II. 1. 34-36.   40. S. B. II. 3. 17.
41 S. B. II. 3. 19-32.

mind, just as the quality of redness is produced in a jar by the conjunction of the jar with fire. Otherwise consciousness would continue to work even in deep sleep, swoon or passion. This is not valid. The essential nature of the soul is eternal intelligence, because it is one with the highest soul, and the highest soul is eternal intelligence. In sleep etc. also the intelligence is alive, but the absence of actual intelligising is due to the absence of objects, not to the absence of intelligence, just as the light pervading the space is not apparent owing to the absence of things to be illuminated, not to the absence of its own nature.[42]

Two features particularly characterise the soul: unity and continuity. Upon this doctrine hinges the fundamental difference between the theory of the *Bauddhas* and Shankara's system. Shankara says: " The philosopher who maintains that all things are momentary only, would have to extend that doctrine to the perceiving person also;

---

42. S. B. II. 3, 18.

that is, however, not possible, on account of the remembrance which is consequent on the original perception. That remembrance can take place only if it belongs to the same persons who previously made the perception; for we observe that what one man has experienced is not remembered by another man." "We admit that sometimes with regard to an external thing a doubt may arise whether it is that or is merely similar to that; for mistakes may be made concerning what lies outside our minds. But the conscious subject has never any doubt whether it is itself or only similar to itself; it rather is distinctly conscious that it is the one and the same subject which yesterday had a certain sensation and to-day remembers that sensation."[43] "Unless there exists *one continuous principle equally connected with the past, the present, and the future, or an absolutely unchangable (Self)* which cognises everything, we are unable to account for remembrance, recognition, and so on,

---

43. S. B. II. 2. 25.

which are subject to mental impressions dependent on place, time, and cause."[44]

The Supreme criterion, which distinguishes the spiritual intelligence-the soul-from all material objects, is that the former can illuminate itself, while the latter cannot shine by their own light but require the aid of an intelligent principle. Matter as such is darkness—negation; its knowability depends upon the soul. " It is quite possible to deny the shining of the sun, the moon and so on with regard to *Brahman* for whatever is perceived is perceived with the light of *Brahman* only, so that the sun, moon etc. can be said to shine in it, while *Brahman* as self-luminous, is not perceived by any other light. *Brahman manifests everything else, but is not manifested by anything else.*"[45] " Form and colour and other qualities do not make their own colour or the colour of something else their objects; the elements and their products on the other hand whether external or belonging to the self (organism) are

---

44. S. B. II. 2. 31.   45. S. B. I. 3. 22.

rendered objects by consciousness."[46] The Self or Intelligence or Reality, therefore, constitutes the ultimate principle which renders knowledge of all things possible, which itself shines in its own light. The Self is distinct from and superior to ideas, because the ideas require an ultimate principle which unites and connects them, while the soul is itself the ultimate principle which renders the cognition of the ideas possible. "The witnessing Self and the idea are of an essentially different nature, and may therefore stand to each other in the relation of knowing subject and object known. The existence of the witnessing Self is self-proved and cannot therefore be denied. Moreover if you maintain that the idea, lamplike manifests itself without standing in need of a further principle, you maintain thereby that ideas exist which are not apprehended by any of the other means of knowledge, and which are without a knowing being ; which is no better than to assert that a thousand lamps burning inside

---
46. S. B. III, 3. 54.

some impenetrable mass of rocks manifest themselves...As the lamp in order to become manifest requires some other intellectual agent furnished with instruments such as the eye, and that therefore the idea also as equally being a thing to be illuminated, becomes manifest only through an ulterior intelligent principle."[47]

It is argued by some people that the soul is active. But the Self's activity is due to its limiting adjuncts and not to its own fundamental nature. For if activity were the nature of the soul, it would be impossible for the soul to be free from it, which means impossibility of final release, because activity is essentially painful. Release also does not depend upon actions; otherwise it will be finite. There is no individual soul apart from the highest soul; and the conditions of activity belong only to the realm of *Maya*.[48]

The individual soul has no reality, no existence apart from the highest soul. "That same highest *Brahman* constitutes — as we

---

47 S. B. II. 2. 28.   48. S. B. II. 3, 33–40.

know from such passages as 'that art thou' —the real nature of the individual soul, while its second nature i. e. that aspect of it which depends on fictitious limiting conditions, is not its real nature."[49] In I. 4. 20, Shankara gives the view of Ashmarathya, known as the *Bhedabhedavada*. The *Bhamati* puts it thus " As the sparks issuing from the fire are not absolutely different from fire, because they participate in the nature of fire, and on the other hand, are not absolutely non-different from the fire, because in that case they could neither be distinguished from the fire, nor from each other ; so the individual souls also, which are effects of *Brahman* are neither absolutely different from *Brahman*, for that would mean that they are not of the nature of intelligence ; nor absolutely non-different from *Brahman*, because in that case they would not be distinguished from each other and because if they were indentical with *Brahman* and therefore omniscient, it would be useless to give them any instruc-

---

49. S. B. I. 3. 19.

tion. Hence the individual souls are somehow different from *Brahman* and somehow non-different."[50] Audulomi advocates what is known as *Satyabhedavada*. "The individual soul is absolutely different from the highest Self; it is inquinated by the contact with its different limiting adjuncts. But it is spoken of in the *Upnishads* as non-different from the highest Self, because after having purified itself by means of knowledge and meditation, it may pass out of the body and become one with the highest Self."[51] Kashakritsna, however, holds that the non-modified highest Lord himself is the individual soul, not anything else. " Only on the opinion of Kashakritsna immortality can be viewed as the result of the knowledge of the soul; while it would be impossible to hold the same view if the soul were a modification (product) of the Self and as such liable to lose its existence by being merged in the causal substance."[52]

---

50. Thibeaut vol. I. p. 277.
51. Thibeaut, vol. I. p. 278.   52. S. B. I. 4. 22.

From the above view also follows the unity of the Self. " As therefore the individual soul and the highest Self differ in name only, it being a settled matter that perfect knowledge has for its object the absolute oneness of the two ; it is senseless to insist (as some do) on a plurality of selves, and to maintain that the individual soul is different from the highest Self and the highest Self from the individual soul. For the Self is indeed called by many different names, but it is one only."[53]

Various objections are raised against these views. " It may be said that as *Brahman* is omnipresent like ether, it follows that *Brahman* also has the same fruition of pleasure, pain, and so on (as the individual soul). The same result follows from its unity." To this it is replied that there is a difference of nature. " For there is a difference between false knowledge and perfect knowledge, fruition being the figment of false knowledge while the unity (of the Self) is revealed by perfect knowledge."[54] The same objection is

---

53. S B. I. 4. 22.   54. S. B. I. 2. 8.

expressed differently. " If we admit that the souls are the parts of the Lord, it follows that the Lord also whose part the soul is, will be affected by the pain caused to the soul by its experience of the *Samsara*-state ...Herefrom it would follow that they who obtain *Brahman* obtain greater pain; so that the former *Samsara*-condition would be preferable and complete knowledge devoid of purpose."55 To this it is replied that all pain is due to illusion and hence the Lord is free from it.56 Again, if there is only one internal Self of all beings, what room is there for permissions and prohibitions, worldly as well as Vedic ? To this it is replied that "injunctions and prohibitions are based on the Self's connection with the body."57 Further, from the admission of the unity of the Self it follows that there must be a confusion of the fruits of actions, there being only one master. " This is not so : (a) For the individual soul depends on its adjuncts, and owing to

---

55. S. B. II. 3. 45. 56. S. B. II. 3. 46.
57. S. B. II. 3. 47-48.

the non-extension of this adjuncts there is also non-extension of the soul. Hence there is no confusion of actions. (b) And that individual soul is to be considered a mere appearance of the highest Self, like the reflexion of the sun in the water ; it is neither directly that nor a different thing. There is therefore, no confusion of actions and results.[58]

The individual soul, in fact, is identical with the highest soul. But owing to connection with *upadhis*—limiting adjuncts (which connection however is illusory), it appears to act. These *upadhis* are (1) the coarse body consisting of the elements ; this is dissolved at death ; (2) other parts accompany the soul through its transmigrations (A) a changing part, viz. moral determination (कर्माश्रय) (B) an unchanging part which disappears only at the time of liberation ; this consists of (a) the subtle body, " the subtle portions of the elements which compose the seed of the body ;" (b) the life organs

---

58. S. B. II, 3, 49–51.

(प्राणाः); these are divided into conscious and unconscious (1) the organs of the conscious life are the (a) five organs of the sense (बुद्धीन्द्रियाणि), sight, hearing, smell, taste, touch (II) five organs of actions (कर्मेन्द्रियाणि) functions of speech, of the hands, the feet, the organs of generation and evacuation; (III) the *manas*, the central organ of conscious life, directing the ten organs. (b) the organ of unconscious life is *prāna* (breath).[59]

We shall not elaborate this further, but note a few interesting points. In the first place, it is to be observed in this system that the soul is separated from all other apparatus " by the whole diameter of being." The soul is the only spiritual principle; all other factors including mind are merely material or non-spiritual. " मनश्चक्षुरादीन्यचेतनानि "[60]. "Mind, eyes etc. are material." This discrimination is made on the principle that the soul is the only source of intelligence; it is self-evident; it shines in its own light. But these organs derive their principle of

---

59. Dr. Deussen, p. 325-6.   60. H. C. 2.

activity and life from the soul; by themselves they are inert and lifeless. Hence the soul is always a subject and never an object; *manas* etc. can be an object of the soul. And it is a cardinal principle of this system that whatever exists for something else, whatever can be an object for a subject is non-intelligent (जड).[61] Even the principle of self-consciousness (अहंप्रत्ययविषयत्व) or अहंकार is non-intelligent, it does not exist in its own right. It is the object of apperception to the soul. " Non-agentship which has self-consciousness for its antecedent belongs to the apperceiving principle (उपलब्धृ-soul); for self-conciousness itself is an object of apperception (on the part of the उपलब्धृ-the pure, isolated, intelligent Self)"[62] What then is the difference between the self-consciousness and the soul ? It is not a mere verbal difference. The self-consciousness (अहंकार) is expressly (अहंप्रत्ययविषय) an object of the consciousness viz. ' I. ' It is the narrow, circumscribed ego,

---

61. H. C. 2. 62. S. B. II. 3. 40.

within us. This ego is not the final key, the master clue to the interpretation of Reality ; hence it cannot be the ultimate principle. We can supplant it by a higher ego, the ego of the universe. A broadening and deepening of the Self within us takes place, till we arrive at the identity of the individual and cosmic consciousness. This cosmic self-consciousness, this common 'I' in all things, this bed-rock of 'I' in each thing or person, is the soul ; it is अस्मत्प्रत्ययविषय. This is the final form which our self-consciousness can attain ; beyond it we cannot go. Hence it can supplant all things, even our narrow egoisms ; but it itself can be supplanted by none. In this sense Shankara insists with persistent emphasis upon the fact that the soul is always a subject and never an object. While it remains identical with the all, it is impossible for it to be an object ; if it becomes an object, it ceases to be a subject. But an object without a subject is an impossibility; hence a pure self-consciousness, feeling itself in complete identity with the soul of the universe is the last and the most ultimate form of being we can conceive. It is only by a narrowing of itself by a voluntary act of self-limitation that the subject can become an object ; but then for that time that object is not pure subject, it is something less than the original state of pure self-consciousness ; so far it is not the pure ultimate *atman*. In this act lies the mystery of the Creation ; the subject surrendering by some mysterious act (called *Maya* in the *Vedanta*) its own state of pure subject-ness and becoming apparently its own object and thus losing a part as it were of its reality. In this way the whole universe (अनात्मन्, —the non-ego) arises ; but the pure self-consciousness still maintains its role of the Being-in-itself or the Absolute ; it keeps up its own identity as a pure साक्षिन् or witnessing principle, above thought, outside activity, beyond appearance and yet the only conceivable source of thought and activity and appearance. The *Vedanta* of Shankara thus approaches closely the theory of Plotinus ; there is a gradual degradation (apparent indeed for Shankara) of the supreme principle. "It can be shown that the Self is extremely pure, extremely clear and extremely subtle. And *Buddhi* (reason) being as pure etc. as the Self, it can put on the semblance of that aspect of the Self which is manifested as consciousness. *Manas* puts on a semblance of *Buddhi*, the sense-organs put on a semblance of *manas*, and the physical body puts on a semblance of the sense-organs. Wherefore common people look upon the mere physical body as the Self."[63]

It has been often said that the Indian thinkers place knowing above willing, that the essence of personality lies for them in intellect rather than in will. But these expressions are rather misleading. The essence of man's self is as much raised above what we ordinarily conceive as intellection or thinking, as above conation or willing. The above quotation clearly shows that *Buddhi* is a higher faculty in psychology than *Manas*. *Buddhi*, in fact, is the nearest

---
63. Bg. C. XVIII. 50; Br. C. IV. 3. 7.

approximation to the core of our self-consciousness. The following quotation also bears out this fact. " Beyond the senses are the sense-objects, beyond sense-objects is *manas*; beyond *manas* is *Buddhi* and beyond *Buddhi* is the great soul."[64] The objects are beyond the senses because the senses are called graspers (ग्रहाः) and the objects are superior to the graspers (अतिग्रहाः). The mind (मनस्) again is superior to the objects, because the relation of the senses and their objects is based on the mind. The *Buddhi* is higher than the mind, because, the objects of enjoyment are conveyed to the soul by means of the *Buddhi*.[65] Now by *manas*, Shankara means the faculty of reflection, and by *Buddhi* the faculty of decision. (निश्चय, अध्यवसाय).[66] Hence in Shankara's psychology, willing is considered a more ultimate and essential part of self than reflection. And if the highest principle is the source of all intelligence, it is also the source of all activity.

---
64. S. B. I. 4. 1.   65. S. B. I. 4. 1.
66. S. B. II. 3. 32, S. B. I. 4. 1.

In fact, it is raised above all ordinary consciousness and is the source of all willing, feeling and knowing. Shankara, therefore, cannot be characterised as an intellectualist any more than he is a voluntarist.

This internal organ is variously called, but Shankara adopts the term *manas* to convey all states of consciousness. " The *manas* has all things for its objects and extends to the past, the present and the future ; it is one only but has various functions."67 The soul is a constant factor ; " hence we have to acknowledge the existence of an internal organ through whose attention and non-attention perception takes place."68 In the commentary on the *Brihadaranyaka*, Shankara gives two proofs of the existence of *manas* : the one is that it is *manas*, which renders all knowledge through senses possible. It is called सर्वकरणविषययोगी. Another proof is the capacity of judgment which we possess. Somebody whom we cannot see touches us ; and we infer the person. Now mere touch

---

67. S. B. II. 4. 6.   68. S. B. II. 3. 32.

cannot make us aware of this fact. The faculty by which we make such an inference is *manas*. [69]

Here it is convenient to refer in brief to the *Adwaita* theory of perception. It is the soul or the *Chaitanya* within us that makes perception possible. " As the existence of the elements and their products is concluded from the fact that they are perceived; so the conclusion must also be drawn that this perception is different from them (perception makes the material world known and not *vice versa*); and perception is just the nature of the soul. " [70] The *Chetana* within us unites with the *Chetana* in the object and the result is perception. It does not therefore follow that mind and senses are useless. The justification of the existence of mind is already given. The senses are necessary for adaptation of perception to their approximate things. " From the soul's essential nature being intelligence, it does not follow that the senses are useless, for they serve

---

69. Br. C. I. 5. 4.   70. S. B. III. 3. 54.

the purpose of determining the special object of each sense such as smell and so on." [71] All errors arise through these intermediate processes.

The immortality of the soul follows logically from the fundamental idealistic position of *Adwaita*. (1) *Moral Argument*. " If the individual soul perishes after the body, there would be no sense in the religious injunctions and prohibitions referring to the enjoyment and avoidance of pleasant and unpleasant things in another body." [72] (1) *Psychological Argument* (a) Apperception is different from the things apperceived; and apperception is the nature of the soul. " Thus the independence of the soul from the body and its eternity follow from the unity of apperception." [73] (b) It also follows from the fact that the self, although connected with a different state, recognises itself as the conscious agent.[74] (2) *Metaphysical Argument*: The identity of the Self with *Brahman* im-

---

71 S. B. II. 3. 18.   72. S. B. II. 3. 166; I. 2, 19.
73. S. B. III. 3. 54.   74. S. B. III. 3. 54.

plies that transcendental existence (independent of time, space and causality) belongs to its essence. 75 Negative arguments are adduced to show that the Self is separate from the body: (a) the qualities of the body, such as form and so on, may be viewed as existing as long as the body exists; life, movement etc. on the other hand, do not exist even when the body exists, viz. in the state of death. (b) the qualities of the body again such as form and so on are perceived by others; not so the qualities of the Self, such as consciousness, remembrance and so on. (c) We can ascertain the presence of the qualities of the Self so long as the body exists; but we cannot ascertain their non-existence when the body does not exist. (d) Elements and their products are objects of consciousness and that hence the latter cannot be a quality of them, as it is contradictory that anything should act on itself. (e) Perceptive consciousness takes place when there are certain auxiliaries such as the

---

75. S. B. II. 3. 17.

lamps and the like, and does not take place where those are absent, without its following therefrom that perception is an attribute of the lamp and the like. Analogously, the fact that perception takes place where there is a body, and does not take place where there is none, does not imply that it is an attribute of the body; for like lamps and so on, the body may be used (by the Self) as a mere auxiliary. (f) Nor is it even true that the body is absolutely required as an auxiliary of perception; for in the state of dream we have manifold perceptions while the body lies motionless. [76]

The state of final liberation is not conceived in a negative way. *Moksha* no doubt means disappearance of all duality, all division of subject and object. But existence and consciousness and bliss remain fundamental. As Hoffding puts it :— " In the mystical concept of God, as well as in the Buddhist concept of *Nirvana*, it is precisely the inexhaustible positivity which bursts

---

76. S. B. III. 3. 53. 54.

through every conceptual form and turns every determination into an impossibility."[77] Names and forms vanish; individual consciousness disappears; but what remains is not a mere negation, but the fulness of existence; fulness of consciousness and fulness of bliss. " पूर्णमेवावशिष्यते । "

---

[77]. Quoted by Ward, Pluralism and Theism p. 35.

CHAPTER IV.

THE DOCTRINE OF MAYA

The doctrine of *Maya* is a very important landmark in the history of philosophic speculation in India. It lies at the root of the sublime structure of the *Adwaita* philosophy. The theory of *Maya* rendered possible a monistic system; and the One without a second was then able to stand aloft in classic majesty and to become the principle of explanation of the whole world. The Hindu sages were convinced from the beginning that the ultimate Reality must be one; that it must be above all birth, growth, decay and death; that it must be infinite, eternal, changeless. Nothing disconcerted them more than the all-pervasive influence of change. The universe was a sort of Heraclitean flux, a perpetual whirl, an eternal shifting of cosmic dust, where nothing *is*, but everything *becomes.* This essentially transitory and perishable nature of all things, even those the most valuable creates a sort of disgust in all minds; and in proportion to the depth and subtlety of nature, this reaction from the world works more or less powerfully in the bosom of every individual or nation. An irresistible feeling rises up that the finite can never satisfy the Infinite within us that the changing and the perishable cannot satisfy the changeless and deathless nature of ours. This is the psychological genesis of the doctrine of *Maya*; and in one shape or another it has obtained a very great hold over humanity. It is the verdict passed by the *Adwaita* philosophy upon all appearance, upon all change.

The crux of all philosophy is said to lie in the relations of the Infinite and the finite, the Absolute and the relative, the One and the many. Religious and metaphysical consciousness in us demands the reality of the former, the ethical and scientific consciousness demands the reality of the latter. Can both be preserved ? *or* should one be swallowed up by the other ?

To reconcile these apparent conflicts, Shankara introduces the conception of grades of reality and truth. Corresponding to the highest Reality there is the highest knowledge. The science of this Reality is Metaphysics. Corresponding to the lower Reality, there is our ordinary knowledge and experience. The science of this Reality is physics (very broadly understood). In fact, there is a fundamental difference between these two points of view. The great merit of Shankara lies in his realizing clearly and acutely that the empirical view of things can never explain the ultimate Reality and hence it is absolutely unsatisfactory. The sphere of this empirical knowledge is the world with all its differences and distinctions. But if empirical knowledge were our only knowledge, metaphysics was impossible, and with it all higher religion and all knowledge of Reality. The result would be agnosticism or materialism. Shankara, however, after sharply pointing out the relative nature of all knowledge based on ordinary experience, established very firmly the foundations of all metaphysics in the possibility we have of transcending ordinary experience and realizing the highest truths. This distinction of standpoints – the empirical and the transcendental view of things – is fundamental in the philosophy of Shankara, and it helps him to solve many difficult problems in his metaphysics.

The first assumption, therefore, of Shankara's philosophy is that there is only one Reality rooted in our self-consciousness and that all other experience is comparatively unreal. The confusion of this distinction is the root of all our experience. " Object (विषय) and subject (विषयिन्) having as their province, the presentation of the ' Thou ' (the not-I) and the ' I, ' are of a nature as opposed as darkness and light. If it is certain that the being of the one is incompatible with the being of the other it follows so much the more that the qualities of the one also do not exist in the other. Hence it follows that the transfer (अध्यास) of the object, and its qualities to the subject and conversely, that the transfer of the subject and its qualities to the object, is logically false,—yet in mankind this procedure resting on false knowledge, of pairing together the true and the untrue (that is subjective and objective) is inborn so that they transfer the being and qualities of the one to the other, not separating object and subject, although they are absolutely different and so saying for example ' This am I ', ' That am I '. " This passage with which Shankara begins his great *Bhashya* is of very great importance inasmuch as it lays down the root of all worldly distinctions and thus points indirectly to the proper goal of metaphysics.

Thus the fundamental fact about the world of experience is its illusory character. It is under the operation of an eternal illusion that we posit the outer world (the not-I) in opposition to the inner world (I). This is called अध्यास. It is defined as :— " the transference of the attributes of one thing to another."[1] "Extra-personal attributes are superimposed on the Self, if a man considers himself sound and entire, or the contrary, as long as his wife, children, and so on are sound and entire or not. Attributes of the body are superimposed on the Self, if a man thinks of himself (his self) as stout, lean, fair, as standing, walking or jumping; attributes of the sense-organs, if he thinks I am mute, or deaf, or one-eyed or blind; attributes of the internal organ, when he considers himself subject to desire, intention, doubt, determination and so on. Thus the producer of the notion of the Ego (i. e. the internal organ) is super-imposed on the interior Self, which in reality is the witness of all the modifications of the internal organ, and *vice versa* the interior Self, which is the witness of everything, is super-imposed on the internal organ, the senses and so on."[2] The opposite of this *Adhyasa* is right know-

---

1. S. B. I. 1. 1.   also (III. 3. 9.), (I. 3. 2)
" अध्यारोपापवादाभ्यां निष्प्रपंचं प्रपञ्च्यते । "
2. S. B. I. Introduction.

ledge; वस्तुस्वरूपावधारणं — the determination of the being in itself of things.

There are two grounds why the empirical view of things is relegated to *Avidya* — the sphere of ignorance. Firstly, because it implies belief in the sense-organs and body as belonging to the Self; and secondly because it is the same as that of animals, who also seek what is desirable and avoid what is undesirable.³

Avidya creates all variety, all differences in the world. It is the source of the Many.⁴ Hence effects apart from their causes, the manifold apart from its underlying substance, are all unreal. The instance of clay is cited. " If there is known a lump of clay which really and truly is nothing but clay, there are known thereby likewise all things made of clay, such as jars, dishes, pails and so on, all which agree in having clay for their true nature. For these modifications or effects are names only, and exist through or originate from speech only, while in reality there

---

3. S. B. 1. Introduction.   4. Bg. C. 13. 13.

exists no such thing as a modification. In so far as they are names (individual effects distinguished by names) they are untrue; in so far as they are clay, they are true."⁵ In the same way, the entire body of effects has no existence apart from *Brahman*. The following reasoning proves the above contention. " The fact of the embodied soul having its self in *Brahman* is self-established, not to be accomplished by endeavour. This doctrine of the individual soul having its self in *Brahman* if once accepted as the doctrine of the *Veda*, does away with the independent existence of the individual soul, just as the idea of the rope does away with the idea of the snake. And if the doctrine of the independent existence of the individual soul has to be set aside, than the entire phenomenal world —which is based on the individual soul —having an independent existence is likewise to be set aside."⁶ This view is open to the following objections (started by the pluralists). (a) " If we

---

5. S. B. II. 1. 14; Bg. C. II. 1   6. 6. S. B. II. 1. 14.

acquiesce in the doctrine of the Absolute unity, the ordinary means of right knowledge, perception etc. become invalid, because the absence of manifoldness deprives them of their objects." (b) "All the texts embodying injunctions and prohibitions will lose their purport if the distinction on which their validity depends does not really exist." (c) "And further the entire body of the doctrine which refers to final release will collapse, if the distinction of teacher and pupil on which it depends is not real. And if the doctrine of release is untrue, how can we maintain the truth of the absolute unity of the Self, which forms an item of that doctrine?" Shankara refutes these objections and at the same time vindicates the comparative reality of the empirical view. "These objections do not damage our position because the entire complex of phenomenal existence is considered as true as long as the knowledge of *Brahman* being the Self of all has not arisen; just as the phantoms of a dream are considered to bs true until the sleeper wakes...Hence, as long as true knowledge does not present itself, there is no reason why the ordinary course of secular and religious activity should not hold on undisturbed." The *Vedanta* texts although untrue can convey true information; as dreams, although unreal often prognosticate real events. Moreover, there is finality as regards the truth of the unity of the Self, hence nothing remains to be desired after it is realised. And this consciousness is neither useless nor erroneous because it results in rooting out nescience; and it cannot be sublated by any other kind of evidence. [7]

It is with very great ingenuity that the nature of *Avidya* is defined. It is the antecedent condition of the world. (प्रागवस्था). It is the potentiality of action. "That causal potentiality is of the nature of nescience; it is rightly denoted by the term 'undeveloped'; it has the highest Lord for its substratum; it is of the nature of an illusion; it is a universal sleep in which are lying the trans-

---
7. S. B. II. 1. 14.

migrating souls destitute for the time of the consciousness of their individual character."[8] It is variously called '*Akasha*', '*Akshara*', '*Maya*'. It is rightly called undeveloped or non-manifested, because it cannot be defined either as that which is or that which is not. " Belonging to the self, as it were, of the omniscient Lord, there are *name* and *form*, the figments of nescience, not to be defined as either being (i. e. *Brahman*) nor as different from it, the germs of the entire expanse of the phenomenal world, called in *Shruti* and *Smriti* the illusion (माया), power (शक्ति) or nature (प्रकृति) of the omniscient Lord."[9] Thus as regards its precise nature nothing can be said; it is neither real nor unreal. It manifests itself as *names* and *forms* (नाम रूपे व्याकरवाणि). " Let me evolve *names* and *forms*." A third factor which goes to constitute the world is *Karman*. The law of causation embraces the whole empirical realm and is thus an essential feature of its consti-

---

8. S. B. I. 4. 3.
9. S. B. II. 1. 14.

tution.¹⁰ " एतदेव हि सर्वं व्याकृतम्– ' त्रयं वा इदं नाम रूपं कर्म ' "

Maya is without beginning (अनादि) and also without end (अनंत), with reference to the *samsara*."¹¹ With regard to an individual, it definitely terminates with the rise of knowledge. It is the source of all modifications and all qualities. " Know thou that all emanations from *Buddhi* down to the physical body, and all qualities, such as those which manifest themselves as pleasure, pain, delusion and other mental states spring from *Prakriti* or *Maya*, composed of the three *gunas*. In fact, if we deduct from existence, the factor of *Brahman* – the one source of all illumination and activity, the rest is *Maya*. Hence *Avidya* or *Maya* is often defined as अनात्मन् or अब्रह्मन् (not-self or non-*Brahman*).¹² *Avidya* is therefore called अचेतन; it has no capacity for action itself.¹³ It is frequently called darkness, because it has no principle of light or intelli-

---

10. Br. C. Introd.   11. S. B. Introduction.
12. Br. C. I. 4. 10.   13. S. B. III. 2. 36.

gence within itself.[14] "The manifestation of this entire world, consisting of names and forms, acts, agents and fruits (of action), has for its cause the existence of the light of *Brahman*, just as the existence of the light of the sun is the cause of the manifestation of all form and colour."[15]

The relations of God and *Avidya*, and *Brahman* and *Avidya* remain to be cleared up. It is frankly acknowledged that it must have a substratum; it cannot hang in the air.[16] It has no independence with reference to God. It is परमेश्वराश्रया.[17] It belongs to the self as it were of the omniscient Lord.[18] It has sprung from the highest Lord.[19] But this dependence of *Maya* upon God or its emanation from Him is true only in the exoteric metaphysics. The pure *Brahman* is not in the least affected by *Avidya*. " As the magician is not at any time affected by the magical illusion produced by himself,

---

14.-15. S. B. I. 3. 22.
16. Br. C. II. 3. 6.   17. S. B. I. 4. 3.
18. S. B. II. 1. 14.   19. S. B. I. 4. 9.

because it is unreal, so the highest Self is not affected by the world-illusion."[20] From the point of view of the Absolute, *Maya* dose not exist at all. "*Maya* is not a reality; it does not exist."[21] The *Adwaita* adopts the theory of absolute non-evolution (अजाति), which is the entire negation of causality.[22]

Nor is *Avidya* inherent in the nature of the soul. " And *Avidya* is cognised by one's own experience; I am ignorant, and my understanding cannot discriminate......... Therefore *Vidya* (knowledge) and *Avidya* (ignorance) should be brought under the categories of name and form. Name and form are certainly not the attributes of the *Atman*."[23] In the commentary on the *Gita* also Shankara lays down that *Avidya* inheres in the organ, not in the Self. " If (false perception etc) were essential properties of the Self, as the heat is an essential property of fire, there could be no getting rid of them at any time; and it is impossible for the

---

20. S. B. II. 1. 9.   21. Ma. C. IV. 58.
22. Ma. C. IV. 59.   23. Ta. C. Vall. Br. VIII. 5.

immutable and formless Self, all-pervading like the *Akasha*, to unite or part with anything whatever."[24]

What is then the explanation of *Avidya*? How does it originate? From the standpoint of the Absolute, such a question has no meaning. "This entire phenomenal world in which good and evil actions are done, is a mere illusion, owing to the non-discrimination of (the Self's) limiting adjuncts, viz. a body and so on, which spring from mere name and form, the presentations of nescience and *does in reality* not exist at all."[25] The pure *Brahman* cannot send forth the illusion at all. Hence *Maya* has no basis in the Absolute. It does not originate by means of a principle of difference in the nature of the Absolute itself. In fact, it has no existence whatever, nor even as an illusion or a dream for the pure spirit. It is in this way that the purest and most rigorous type of monism was reached. *Maya* or *Avidya* has no existence independent or dependent in a

---

24. Bg. C. XIII. 2. 25. S. B. II, 1. 22.

scheme of pure metaphysics. It cannot therefore affect the monistic character of the *Adwaita* philosophy. It is of the nature of darkness or negation; and how can he who is in the atmosphere of pure light perceive darkness at all? A sudden stroke of mystic illumination puts an end to all our empirical existence altogether, and the very idea or remembrance of such a thing as this world of ours or the narrow individuality of the spirit in this world, absolutely leaves the Self.

True, illusion even as an illusion must be accounted for. Hence from the *Vyahavarika* point of view we may try to explain its origin and nature. The seat of *Avidya* is in the mind of man. The explanation of the empirical concept must be sought in the nature of our cognitive faculty. Shankara, to a certain extent, explains *Avidya* in this way. It is called नैसर्गिक; it is innate in our mental faculty. It is मिथ्याज्ञाननिमित्त, based on wrong knowledge; and knowledge is a function of the mind. It is मिथ्याप्रत्ययरूप, it consists in the form of a wrong conception. " All *jiwas* —human entities—which are really non-existent, are (with all concomitant appearance of birth, death etc) mere results of the objectivising tendency, of the mind and nothing else."[26] " The whole experience i. e. duality made up of perceiver and perceived, is pure imagination."[27] "There is no *Avidya* apart from the mind...on its destruction all is destroyed ; its activity is the cause of all appearance."[28]

Avidya works through उपाधिs (attributes, determinations, limiting adjuncts). All the special apparatus required by *Avidya* constitute the *Upadhis* of the soul. Mind is an *Upadhi*, *buddhi* is an *Upadhi*, *ahamkara* is an *Upadhi*, and so on. *Upadhi*, therefore, is the product of *Avidya*. " The limiting adjuncts are presented by nescience only."[29]

Such is the account of the famous doctrine of *Maya* as elaborated by Shankara. The verdict which this theory passes upon all our

---

26. Ma. C. IV. 70.   27. Ma. C. IV. 72.
28. V. 171.   29. S. B. III. 2. 11.

very dear things, upon our worldly ambitions, upon all our literary, scientific, and philosophical activities, upon our ethical and religious aspirations, upon our political and social ideals, upon our inmost loves, in short upon our God, nature and our very existence as individuals among other individuals, is a ruthless and sweeping one. One stroke of the pen of the *Vedantin* seems to be effectual in sending to the gallows the whole existence. There is something very sublime indeed in these flights of our metaphysical imagination, in which we leave behind all our illusions — illusions which we hug to our bosoms and illusions which we fly from, illusions pleasant and painful — the illusion of the outer world, the illusion of thought, the illusion of God and the illusion of our individual existence, till we reach the Absolute It requires a very robust metaphysical capacity in man to face all these ordeals. Hard thinking, persistent thinking, clear thinking, thinking to the roots of all problems, to the very fundamentals of all situations, to the very presuppositions of all thought and being, is the very essence of metaphysics. He who has no courage to face the results of his thinking, to swallow the conclusions of his thought, whatever they may mean to him personally, should never take the trouble to philosophise.

An absolutist philosophy indeed demands very heavy sacrifices. But its conclusion is proportionately splendid. The end justifies the means. It is limitless existence, limitless happiness we get. But after all, even this world dose not disappear as absolutely as is supposed. Thus Ward says : " In the flights of pure thought upto the Absolute the atmosphere of empirical fact by which it is sustained is too diffused to be detected, and when their summit is reached, the particular, the many of actual experience tend to disappear or to be explained away."[30] The tendency cannot be denied ; empirical world, in fact, ceases to exist. But this does not mean annihilation. It merely means that existence changes its form and colour as it were for

---

30. Ward : Pluralism and Theism, p. 23.

the Absolute. It is *empirical* existence and not all existence which vanishes. Existence, Reality, remains. But its limited forms vanish. For a nature which is essentially timeless, and spaceless, temporal and spatial things must change their aspect. All the limitations of our sensation, perception, intelligence and willing cannot inhere in an absolute intelligence. Thus externality has to go, difference between subject and object has to go, spatial and temporal views of things must go, causal determination of one thing by another must go, maniness as well as oneness must go. This is inevitable. But the universe with all its reality will not go, even for the liberated soul. It will merely change its form, meaning, and significance. Nothing will disappear except a false view, a limited horizon, an erroneous idea, a circumscribed vision. Fact, Reality, Existence, however will remain as fundamental as ever. But the view-point will change. This is the radical change which the *Vedanta* claims to work in our intelligence.

"Our highest knowledge must suffer an entire transformation if — while preserving its value — it is to be absorbed into the highest, most all-embracing totality that we can conceive."[31] It never means to affect Reality at all. It only means to take away the form which Reality puts on for us, the garment which it wears, the appearance which it assumes and substitute for it Reality in itself without any limiting adjuncts. The greatest of all revolutions then will be the revolution in the standpoint of human intelligence;[32] and that revolution will bring about the downfall of phenomena and the installation of noumena in their stead.

---

31. Hoffding : Philosophy of Religion. p. 86.
32. " दृष्टिं ज्ञानमयीं कृत्वा पश्येद्ब्रह्ममयं जगत् । " शंकर.

CHAPTER V

ETHICAL CONCEPTIONS IN ADWAITISM.

The predominant idea of Shankara's philosophy is metaphysical. It is the nature of what a man is, not what a man should do which interests him most. The original impulse is practical indeed; but this does not mean that the philosophy primarily refers to either ordinary experience or to the interests of science, or to ethical interests. It only means that Shankara cares more for deliverance from worldly existence than for any speculative consistency or wholeness in his ultimate philosophy. Ethics is, therefore, a subordinate department in the system of Shankara. Metaphysics is the primary affair; ethics is purely secondary. Knowledge of Reality is mainly aimed at; practice of morality has value so far as it leads to knowledge of Reality. Ethics, therefore, has no fundamental significance; it has instrumental value only.

The attainment of *Moksha*, the liberation from all empirical existence is the main end of human life. It is thus defined: " But this (*Moksha*) is eternal in the true sense i. e. eternal without undergoing any changes, omnipresent as ether, free from all modifications, absolutely self-sufficient, not composed of parts, of self-luminous nature. That bodiless entity, in fact to which merit and demerit with their consequences and three-fold time do not apply is called release."[1] In brief, it is nothing but the identification with *Brahman*. (" ब्रह्मभावत्वमोक्षः ") Such is the *sumum bonum* in this philosophy.

The very nature of the goal to a certain extent determines the means to be followed. Liberation is not a state to be accomplished or a thing to be obtained.[2] (1) Release is not something to be accomplished. Other-

---
1. S. B. I. 1. 4
2. The main arguments are taken from the Introduction to S. B.

wise it would depend on the action of mind, speech or body. Nor is liberation a mere modification. " Non-eternality of release is the certain consequence of these two opinions; for we observe in common life that things which are modifications, such as sour milk and the like, and the things which are effects, such as jars etc. are non-eternal. " Hence *Brahman* cannot be considered as supplementary to certain actions and release as there effect. Because that release is something eternal is acknowledged by all who admit it at all. (2) Release is not something to be obtained, because it constitutes a person's Self, it is not something to be obtained by that person. And even if *Brahman* were altogether different from a person's Self, still it would not be something to be obtained, for as it is omnipresent, it is part of its nature that it is ever-present to every one, just as ether is. (3) If it is said that release is a quality of Self which is merely hidden and becomes manifest on the Self being purified by some actions ; just as quality of clearness becomes manifest in a mirror when mirror is cleansed by means of the action of rubbing. This objection is invalid, because the Self cannot be the abode of any action. For action cannot exist without modifying that in which it abides. But if the Self were modified by an action, its non-eternity would result therefrom, and texts such as the following 'Unchangeable he is called,' would thus be stultified. Nor can the Self be purified by actions abiding in something else as it stands in no relation to that extraneous something. (4) Liberation is not attainable by (moral) purification (संस्कार). For all improvement takes place in him who is to be purified by the addition of virtues or the diminution of faults. Liberation does not come about by the addition of virtues ; for it consists in identity with *Brahman*, who is incapable of any augmentation of perfection; just as little by diminution of faults ; for *Brahman* is eternally pure.[3] (5) It cannot be an effect of meditation. " That which is

---

3. Dr. Deussen, p. 403.

not proclaimed by speech, by which speech is proclaimed, that only know to be *Brahman*, not that on which people devoutly meditate as this." (6) It cannot be an object of the activity of knowing; because "it is different from the known and again above the unknown." The knowledge of *Brahman* does not therefore, depend on the active energy of man, but is analogous to the knowledge of those things which are the objects of perception etc. and this depends on the object of knowledge only. (7) Release follows immediately on the cognition of *Brahman*; no effect intervenes between the two, "He who knows *Brahman* becomes *Brahman*." (8) There is a fundamental difference between the results of actions and of the knowledge of *Brahman*. From the former accrue pleasure and pain; these are transitory. But a liberated man becomes free from all pleasure and pain. Hence release cannot be the effect of religious merit. (9) Works cannot lead to liberation, because they lead to consequences good or bad in the next existence,

Hence they take us back to *Samsara* and not delieverance from it. As Dr. Deussen puts it : " Liberation, if it were dependent upon works, would necessarily be (1) transitory (owing to the consumption of the works), (2) graduated (because of their different value); both of which contradict the conception of liberation as an eternal and paramount condition."[4] (10) The fruit of knowledge is different from the fruit of work ; the former is produced simultaneously with knowledge ; while the latter is often produced in the future.[5]

On grounds such as these it is established that mere works can never lead to *Moksha*. It is ज्ञान (knowledge) alone which is effective in putting an end to *Samsara*, not ordinary knowledge, nor scientific knowledge, but true philosophic knowledge of the unity of the soul and its identity with *Brahman*. Knowledge alone is sufficient without works ; because liberation is nothing but perfect knowledge. (अम्यग्दर्शन). " फलं च मोक्षोऽ विद्यानिवृत्तिर्वा "

---

4. Dr. Deussen, p. 403.　　5. S. B. III. 4. 15.

"Liberation is nothing but the removal of अविद्या or ignorance."⁶ "ईश्वरस्वरूपापरिज्ञानाद्वन्धः etc."⁷ "Ignorance of the nature of God is bondage; a knowledge of His nature leads to liberation."

It is true that the knowledge of *Brahman* is unlike all other knowledge. It is unlike all empirical knowledge, inasmuch as in the latter, some object is to be discovered; whereas here it is the eternal subject that is the object of investigation. The knower has to become known. But to achieve this, ordinary experience which posits a dualism of subject and object is ineffectual. " He who knows not alone doth know it." The Self in fact, must be turned from all outside activity, all empirical pursuits, towards itself. No effort of understanding or will, no scriptural instruction can take us into the kingdom of the Absolute. As soon as the *avidya* (ignorance) disappears, the Self automatically reveals itself.

The question then arises as to the signifi-

---

6. Br. Up. C. 7. S. B. IV. 2. 5.

cance of ethics in Shankara's system. Morality is not an end in itself; man's business here does not end in making of him an ethically perfect being. Morality is not even a direct means to the end; knowledge of the Self is the one essential for *Moksha*. Is morality then a complete superfluity — the existence or absence of which should be a matter of no account to us? The fact is that we are apt to understand the term ज्ञान or knowledge too abstractly in the light of modern psychology. ज्ञान or knowledge is not a purely intellectual cognition; it has its basis in will, as well. It is an attitude of the soul towards Reality. It is very remote from a verbal superficial insight into the language of the *Vedanta*. A man may delight in the the conundrums of *Vedanta*, may revel in these speculations as intellectual luxuries but he may be a complete ignoramus all the same.

कुशला ब्रह्मवार्तायां वृत्तिहीनाः सुरागिणः । तेप्यज्ञानितमां नूनं पुनरायान्ति यान्ति च ॥ 8

In the commentary on the *Gita*, Shankara

---

8. अपरोक्षानुभूति. 133.

distingushes between a ज्ञानी (one who knows) and तत्त्वदर्शी (one who has realised the truth) "ज्ञानवन्तोऽपि केचन यथावत् तत्त्वदर्शनशीलाः; अपरे न ; ततो विशिनष्टि तत्त्वदर्शिनः इति" [9] What is necessary for liberation is not a mere change in the view of things. It is the turning of the eye of the soul that is necessary: the very fundamental attitude of one's knowing, feeling, willing Self that is to be revolutionised. ज्ञान or knowledge includes willing as an important element in it ; it includes भक्ति or devotion as a substantial part of it ; it is in Bergson's pregnant language *"integral experience."* It is an all-round realization involving in it, a complete conversion of the whole consciousness.

To secure this right and firm attitude of of the soul, it is necessary to go through not only intellectual training, but moral discipline as well. The ethical as well as religious duties have thus an auxiliary value. In the words of Dr. Deussen " Their *role* in the scheme of salvation is not so much *meritorious* as *ascetic*." [10] They are not abso-

---

9. Bg. C. IV. 34.   10. Dr. Deussen: p. 411.

lutely necessary, but they have some value all the same. " Knowledge has regard for all works enjoined on the *ashramas*, and there is no absolute non-regard...knowledge having once sprung up requires no help towards the accomplishment of its fruit, but it does stand in need of something else with a view to its origination."¹¹ Purification is the object of actions; with the attainment of moral purification knowledge becomes possible.¹²

चित्तस्य शुद्धये कर्म न तु वस्तूपलब्धये ।
वस्तुसिद्धिर्विचारेण न किंचित् कर्मकोटिभिः ॥

For people who cannot go through *ashramas* through lack of means, these may be dispensed with.

In the beginning of the *Bhashya*, certain qualifications are laid down for the student of this highest philosophy. These are the essential prerequisites in all cases, without which it is not possible to get the highest knowledge. Religious duties may be ignored; but these factors must be taken into account.

---

11. S. B. III. 4. 26. 12. Vivekachudamani.

"तेषु हि सत्सु प्रागपि धर्मजिज्ञासायां ऊर्ध्वं च शक्यते ब्रह्म जिज्ञासितुं ज्ञातुं च न विपर्यये" (I.I.1.) The first essential is the knowledge of the *Vedas*. "Scripture is the source of cause i. e. the means of right knowledge through which we understand the nature of *Brahman*." Accordingly *Shudras* are debarred from the study of the *Vedanta*. "The *Shudras* are disqualified for that reason also that *Smriti* prohibits their hearing the *Vedas* and their understanding and performing the Vedic mantras." (न शूद्राय मतिं दद्यात्।) Still even in their cases if once knowledge is produced in consequence of after effects of former deeds, the fruit of the knowledge cannot be withheld. Further, a list of qualifications is drawn up for the students of philosophy. I. नित्यानित्यवस्तुविवेकः A sense of discrimination between eternal and non-eternal things. It is defined in the *Vivekachudamani*: "ब्रह्म सत्यं जगन्मिथ्येत्येव रूपो विनिश्चयः" This is the dawn of the metaphysical consciousness in man. II इहामुत्रार्थभोगविरागः A renunciation of the enjoyment of reward here and hereafter. A man must feel the profoundly unsatisfactory character of all finite enjoyments, before he can profit by the teachings of the *Vedanta*. A sacrifice of all personal longings is demanded in order to attain a pure, lofty, unprejudiced view of the ultimate essence. VII शमदमादिसाधनसंपत्: These comprehend together complete peace of mind; freedom from external and internal agitation. उपरति: is defined as "complete renunciation of all desires." तितिक्षा is defined as "Endurance without protest of all sufferings." श्रद्धा is faith "शास्त्रस्य गुरुवाक्यस्य सत्यबुद्ध्यावधारणं "[13] a general faith in the teachings of scriptures and *gurus*; समाधान: concentration and not चित्तस्य लालनं : fondling of the mind.[14] A complete detachment from the outward things, the manifold of sense, together with a capacity for metaphysical abstraction and concentration on inward things are demanded. The voice of the pure spirit cannot be heard till all superficial organs cease to speak. Such a hard system of gymnastic exercises is required of an

---

13. Ibid.   14. Ibid.

earnest seeker after truth. IV. Lastly there is मुमुक्षत्व-a keen sense of the vanity of the world and eagerness to be free from it.

The practice of duties in the *ashramas* is considered as an indirect (बाह्य) means, while calmness of mind etc are the direct means to the realisation of knowledge. The practice of religious duties helps one by removing such obstructions as passions and the like.[15] Further, a childlike state is enjoined on a Brahmin who has done with learning. " He whom nobody knows either as noble or ignoble, as ignorant or learned, as well-conducted, or ill-conducted, he is a *Brahmin*. Quietly devoted to his duty, let the wise man pass through life unknown ; let him sleep on earth as if he were blind, unconscious, deaf."[16] The result of these works may appear now or in the next life. When the means of knowledge which is operative is not obstructed by some other work, the results of which are just then reaching maturity, knowledge already attains maturity in this life;

---

15. S. B. III. 4. 35. 16. S. B. III. 4. 50.

but when such an obstruction takes place then in the next life. And a work's reaching maturity depends on place, time and operative cause presenting themselves.[17]

The question still remains; How is the passage from the finite to the Infinite possible ? The works are important as regards this; the *Shastras* can only remove hindrances and attune the soul to the knowledge of Reality. But ultimately even the knowledge derived from *Shastras* with its necessary polarization into subject and object, is itself a delusion and a snare. How then are we to break these hedges and peep into the Absolute ? From the point of view of the esoteric metaphysics such a question cannot arise ; we leave behind us the category of causality. But an answer is made in the exoteric sphere. It is through the conception of grace that the problem is solved. " The *Samsara* state in which it (the individual soul) appears as agent and enjoyer is brought about *through the permission of the Lord*...

---

17. S. B. III. 4. 51.

and we must therefore assume that final release also is effected through knowledge caused *by the grace of the Lord.*"[18] " In the case of some persons indeed who strenuously meditate on the Lord and who, their ignorance being dispelled at last, obtain *through the favour of the Lord* extraordinary powers and insight— just as through the action of strong medicines the power of sight of a blind man becomes manifest ; but it does not on its own account reveal itself through all men. "[19]

We have discussed so far the role of knowledge and works in a scheme of salvation, which the *Vedanta* offers. We will now see more minutely the nature and significance of morality in the absolutist metaphysics of Shankara. All morality as well as immorality originate in an erroneous view of the would. " Passages such as 'He is to approach his wife at the proper time' and 'He is not to approach the wife of his *Guru*' are examples of permissions (or injunctions) and prohibitions;

---

18. S. B. II. 3. 40.   19. S. B. III. 2. 5.

or again, such passages as 'He is to kill the animal devoted to *Agni* and *Soma*' and 'He is not to hurt any being.' Corresponding examples from ordinary life are; 'A friend is to be served' and 'Enemies are to be shunned'. Permissions and prohibitions of this kind are possible, because the Self although one is connected with various bodies— of what kind then is that connection ? It consists in the origination in the Self of the erroneous notion that the Self is the aggregate consisting of the body and so on. This erroneous notion is to prevail in all beings, and finds its expression in thoughts such as the following. ' I go, ' ' I come, ' ' I am blind, ' ' I am confused. ' This erroneous notion cannot be removed by anything but perfect knowledge and before the latter supervenes, it remains spread among all living beings. And thus, although the Self must be admitted to be one only, injunctions and prohibitions are possible owing to the difference effected by its connection with bodies, and other limiting adjuncts, the products of nescience." [20] In the commentary on the *Gita* also Shankara lays bare the egoistic basis of all morality and immorality. "स्वधर्मे प्रवृत्तानामपि तेषां वाङ्मनःकायादीनां प्रवृत्तिः फलाभिसंधिपूर्वकैव साहंकारा च भवति ।" [21] "Even if they (men under worldly delusions) are devoted to the performance of duty, their conduct in speech, thought and deed is egoistic and is prompted by a longing for reward." "He who knows the truth does not think 'I act;' nor does he long for the results."

The problem of evil does not prove very troublesome to Shankara. Absolutist philosophies generally have a tendency to deny the reality of Evil. The Ultimate of ultimates is necessarily above all good and evil. Evil like the good is only a temporary phase of the world, an accident of our empirical existence, an outcome of a very limited point of view of ours. It has no place in the Absolute.

" The soul being engrossed by nescience identifies itself as it were with the body and

---

20. S. B. II. 3. 48.   21. Bg. C. II. 1 10.

so on and imagines itself to be affected by the experience of pain which is due to nescience. ' I am affected by the pain due to the body '... The pain of the individual soul also is not real, but imaginary only, caused by the error consisting in the non-discrimination of (the Self from) the body, senses, and other limiting adjuncts, which are due to name and form, the effects of nescience. And as a person feels the pain of a burn or cut which affects his body by erroneously identifying himself with the latter, so also he feels also the pain affecting others, such as sons and friends ; by erroneously identifying himself with them entering into them as it were through love, and imagining ' I am the son, I am the friend. ' wherefore we feel with certainty that the feeling of pain is due merely to the error of false imagination. At the same conclusion we arrive on the ground of negative instances. Let us consider the case of many men, each of whom possesses sons, friends etc... while others do not. If then somebody calls out 'the son has died', the 'friend has died', grief is produced in the minds of those who are under the imagination of being connected with sons and friends, but not in the minds of religious mendicants who have freed themselves from the imagination."[22] The same point, viz. the illusory nature of all pain and suffering is brought out in the Introduction. " For we indeed observe that a person who imagines the body and so on, to constitute the Self, is subject to fear and pain, but we have no right to assume that the same person, after having by means of the *Veda*, comprehended **Brahman** to be the Self, and having thus got over his former imaginings, will still in the same manner be subject to pain and fear, whose cause is wrong knowledge. In the same way we see a rich householder puffed up by the conceit of his wealth is grieved when his possessions are taken from him; but we do not see that the loss of his wealth equally grieves him after he has once retired from the world and put off the conceit of

---

[22] S. B. II. 3. 46.

his riches. And again we see that a person possessing a pair of beautiful earrings derives pleasure from the proud conceit of ownership; but after he has lost the earrings and the conceit established thereon, the pleasure derived from them vanishes. Thus *Shruti* also says " When he is free from the body, neither pleasure, nor pain touches him."[23]

Now we may ask the question, how far God is responsible for evil? Two answers are given; in the one the solution of the problem is given up as presenting no special difficulty; in the other, men are held partly responsible for evil. In the pure metaphysics, however as we have seen that the very existence of evil is denied. We will take up the former position first. This solution ignores completely what constitutes in the modern eyes, the sting of the problem. "As among minerals, which are all mere manifestations of earth, nevertheless great variety is observed, some being precious gems, such as diamonds, etc. others such as crystals and the

---

23. S. B. I. 1. 4. (also IV. 1. 2)

ETHICAL CONCEPTIONS

like, being the medium size, and others again stones only fit to be flung on dogs or crows; and as from seeds which are placed on one and the same ground various plants are seen to spring, such as sandal woods and cucumbers, which show the greatest difference in their leaves, blossoms, fruits, fragrance, juice etc. and as the one and the same food produces various effects such as blood and hair; so the one *Brahman* may also produce various effects."[24]

In the following quotations from *Shrutis*, God is plainly made the author of evil: "एष ह्येव साधु कर्म कारयति तं यमेभ्यो लोकेभ्य उन्निनीषते । एष उ एवासाधु कर्म कारयति तं यमधो निनीषते" He makes him whom he wishes to lead up from these worlds do a good deed, and the same makes him whom he wishes to lead down from these worlds to do a bad deed.[25] Also: "स न साधुना कर्मणा भूयान्नो एवासाधुना कनीयान्"[26]

In another passage, Shankara attempts to

---

24. S. B. II. 1. 23.
25. S. B. III. 2. 41 ; II. 1. 34.
26. S. B. I. 3. 43.

free God from the responsibility of creating evil, inasmuch as he does not work arbitrarily, but apportions happiness and misery according to the merits and demerits of man. "The Lord, it is said, cannot be the cause of the world, because, on that hypothesis, the reproach of inequality of dispensation and cruelty ("वैषम्यनैर्घृण्य") would attach to him. Some beings, viz. the gods he renders eminently happy; others, as for instance the animals, eminently unhappy; to some again, as for instance, he allots an intermediate position. To a Lord bringing about such an unequal condition of things, passion and malice would have to be ascribed, just as to any common person acting similarly; which attributes would be contrary to the essential goodness of the Lord affirmed by *Shruti* and *Smriti*. Moreover, as the infliction of pain and the final destruction of all creatures would form part of his dispensation, he would have to be taxed with great cruelty, a quality abhorred by low people even.

The Lord, we reply, cannot be reproached

with the inequality of dispensation and cruelty, ' because he is bound by regards. ' If the Lord on his own account, without any extraneous regards produced this unequal creation, he would expose himself to blame; but the fact is, that in creating he is bound by certain regards, i. e. he has to look to merit and demerit of the living creatures created. It is not a fault for which the Lord is to blame. The position of the Lord is to be looked on as analogous to that of *Parjanya*, the giver of the rain. For as *Parjanya* is the common cause of the production of rice, barley, and other plants, while the difference between the various species is due to the various potentialities lying hidden in the respective seeds, so that the Lord is the common cause of the creation of gods, men etc. While the differences between these classes of beings are due to the different merits belonging to the individual souls. " [27]

An objection is raised as to how God is

---

[27]. S. B. II. I. 34.

guided at the time of creation, when there was no merit and demerit? To this it is replied that as the world is without beginning, merit and inequality are like seed and sprout, caused as well as causes.[28]

The problem whether individuals are free to act or are absolutely bound hand and foot to circumstances has in Shankara's systems, like other problems, a two-fold aspect. Activity is not a characteristic of the ultimate Reality. It is essentially painful and finite. "The Self being an agent cannot be founded on its real nature, because (if it were so) the impossibility of final release will follow. For if being an agent belongs to the soul's nature, it can never free itself from it — no more than fire can divest itself of heat, and as long as man has not freed himself from activity he cannot obtain his highest end, since activity is essentially painful."[29] Another argument is that activity belongs to a finite object. Activity depends on the employment of means and whatever depends on

---

28. S. B. II. 1. 35. 29. S. B. II. 3. 40.

means to be employed is of a non-eternal nature.[30] Activity further argues imperfection in the agent. "Experience shows that all agents, whether they be active for their own purposes or for the purposes of something else, are impelled to action by some imperfection."[31]

The Self is changeless; because it has no parts; for whatever has no parts; is never found to undergo change. Because the Self is changeless, it is unchangeable. (निरवयवत्वाच्च अविक्रियः । नहि निरवयवं कांचित् विक्रियात्मकं दृष्टं । अविक्रियत्वात् अविकार्यः अयम् आत्मा उच्यते ।;[32] The immutability of the Self has given us the reason for the absence of all actions. (उक्त एव आत्मनः अविक्रियत्वं सर्वकर्मासंभवकारणविशेषः)[33] Moreover, " the Self can impossibly become an agent, as it cannot enter into intimate relation to actions. If it should be said that the Self may be considered as an agent in the same way as kings and other great people are (who without acting make others act by their

---

30. S. B. II. 3. 40.   31. S. B. II. 2. 37.
32. Bg. 2. 25.   33. Bg. 2. 21.

presence) we deny the appositeness of this instance; for kings may become agents through their relations to servants whom they procure by giving them wages, &c. While it is impossible to imagine anything analogous to money, which could be the cause of a connection between the Self as Lord and the body and so on (as servants)."[34] Further the soul is all-pervading; and as such no movement is possible in it or of it. " नहि विभोः श्चलनमवकम्पत इति । "[35] " Movement is impossible in the case of all-pervading being." Lastly, a thing cannot be the object of its activity, as fire cannot burn itself."[36]

Activity, therefore, is not a characteristic of *Brahman*; but it is due to *Avidya*.[37] " Wherefore works are enjoined on the ignorant, not on the wise. Before the dawn of wisdom nescience presents itself in various forms — as actions, means and results and becomes the source of all action."[38]

From the standpoint of *Avidya* therefore

---

34. S. B. I. 1. 4.   35. S. B. II. 3. 19.
36. S. B. II. 2. 28.   37. S. B. II. 3. 40.
38. Bg. C. 2. 69.

activity and its results good or bad exist. How can the activity of individual soul be reconciled with the omnipotence of God? The ultimate dependence of all activity upon God is clearly recognised. "For although the soul has its own imperfections such as passion and so on for motives, and although ordinary experience does not show that the Lord is a cause in occupations such as ploughing and the like, yet we ascertain from scriptures that the Lord is a causal agent in all activity. For the scripture says: "He makes him whom he wishes to lead up from these worlds to do a good deed; and the same makes him whom he wishes to lead down from these good worlds, do a bad deed." [39] "Scripture represents the Lord not only as the giver of all fruits but also as the causal agent with reference to all actions whether good or evil."[40] But if the Lord is the cause of all actions, the soul has to undergo consequences for what it has not done. "The Lord makes the soul act, having regard

---

39. S. B. II. 3. 44.   40. S. B. III. 2. 41.

to the efforts made by it, whether meritorious or non-meritorious...The Lord acts as a mere occasional cause...He arranges favourable or unfavourable circumstances for the souls with a view to their former efforts...Although the activity of the soul is not independent. The Lord indeed causes it to act (कारयति), but it acts (करोति) itself. Moreover the Lord in causing it to act now has regard to its former effects, and the caused act in a former existence, having regard to its efforts previous to that existence ; a *regressus* against which, considering the eternity of the *Samsara*, no objections can be raised. But how is it known that Lord has regard to the efforts made (in former existences) ? The *Sutra* replies from the purportlessness etc. of injunctions and prohibitions... On the other alternative they would be without purport, and the Lord in fact would be enjoined in the place of injunctions and prohibitions, since the soul would be absolutely dependent. And, the Lord might requite with evil those who act according to the injunctions, and with good, men doing what is forbidden; which would subvert the authoritativeness, of the *Veda*. Moreover if the Lord were absolutely without any regard, it would follow that also the ordinary efforts of men are without any purport; and so likewise the special conditions of the place, time, and cause."[41]

This discussion clearly brings out that Shankara is fully conscious of three facts; (1) religious consciousness requires that God should be the author of all actions in the world; His omnipotence must be preserved. (2) Science as well as ordinary experience require that causation must have unrestricted sway over the whole world. (3) Morality requires that freedom of man and his responsibility should be recognised. Law and ethics are based upon this postulate. Individual freedom must be retained, and yet the reign of Law must be recognised. Omnipotence of God must exist side by side with these. To reconcile these somewhat contradictory aspects of the situation, the dogma of the beginning-

---

41. S. B. II. 3. 42.

lessness of the *Samsara* is invoked. The solutions of the problems of free will and of evil are made to depend upon this basis. Men's actions indeed are subject to the law of causation. His actions form a sort of geometrical series in which each one follows the preceding ones with mathematical necessity. A man's action is never 'shot out of a pistol'; it is not an inexplicable whim of a mysterious freedom of will. It is merely a link in the chain of causes and effects. Every action of man is a part of the eternal procession of events called *Samsara* and as such has its place there determined by the laws of the *Samsara*. The great law of *Samsara* is the law of Karma. It is the one bond which regulates the evolution or devolution of the universe as a whole or its individual items. " As the tree is evolved out of a seed so also the world is evolved under the operation of the *Karman* of all creatures. "[42] Man in the state of *Avidya* (nescience) is subject to this law and as such

---

42. Br. C. I. Introduction.

he is a part of the material world. A man cannot act independently of this law in the phenomenal world. Karma is often represented as a form of bondage. 43 (कर्मणा बध्यते जन्तुर्विद्यया तु प्रमुच्यते ।) ('लोकोऽयं कर्मबंधनः') " The multitude of beings comprising those that move as well as those that do not move ...involuntarily comes into being at the coming on of day and is dissolved again at the close of the day."43 A

How then can the independence of man be preserved ? Is it a complete fiction ? Has man no autonomy whatsoever ? In the realm of *Avidya*, what we call freedom of will consists in attributing to our own agency the actions which we do. " That the primeval natural nescience leaves room for all practical life or activity—whether worldly or that based on the *Veda*— we have explained more than once."44 All individuality which we attribute to ourselves is due to *Avidya*. 45 The sense of individuality in us is called

---

43. Mahabharata.   43. A. Bg. c. 4. 4. 2.
44. S. B. III. 2. 15.   45. S. B. III. 4. 8.

Ahamkara, and this is the root of all actions. "अहंकार एष हि सर्वस्य प्रवृत्तिबीजं दृष्टं लोके" 46 This consciousness of autonomy is however an illusion even in empirical sphere. "It is by *gunas* or the modifications of *Prakriti*, manifesting themselves as the body and the senses, that all our actions, conducive to temporal and spiritual ends, are done. The man whose mind is variously divided by *Ahamkara*, by egoism, identifying the aggregate of the body and the senses with the Self i. e. who ascribes to himself all the attributes of the body and the senses and thus thoroughly identifies himself with them— he, by nescience, sees actions in himself; as regards every action, he thinks 'I am the doer'. But he who is versed in the classification of the energies (*gunas*) and their respective functions holds that the energies as sense-organs move amid the energies as sense-objects, but not the Self." 47

Shankara is fully alive to the necessity of somehow establishing man's freedom to a

---

46. Bg. C. VII. 4.   47. Bg. C. III. 27-28.

certain extent. If man were denied all initiative, if he be a mere tool in the hands of nature, all morality will be at an end. If man were swallowed up either in God or in nature there would be an end to all responsible life. The whole science of ethics with its " Thou shalt " and " Thou shalt not " will lose all its validity. (" ततश्च प्रामाण्यं वेदस्या-स्तमियात् । ") Human effort will lose all significance, because arbitrary fiats of God and nature will take place of moral sanctions, moral rewards and punishments. (" लौकिक स्यापि पुरुषकारस्य वैयर्थ्यं । ") [48] The result will be a complete chaos. Hence man's responsibility and freedom of will must be preserved. Man can act. (करोति). Freedom of his actions does not mean the absence of their determination by previous antecedents. But then these previous antecedents are not external causes; they do not belong to any outside agency ; they are his own actions in a previous birth ; and these are due to actions more

---

48. S. B. II. 3. 42;

previous still and so on *ad infinitum*, because there is no commencement in this series.

What is the scope for God ? It is clearly recognised that everything, every action, is ultimately due to the agency of God; there is nothing outside the scope of His omnipotence. ("सर्वास्वेव प्रवृत्तिष्वीश्वरो हेतुकर्तेति श्रुतेरवसीयते")[49] The whole series of causes and effects is contrived by God; it has its ultimate ground in God. God indeed cannot make any result arise from any act; but then it is God who makes a particular result spring from a particular cause. God is, therefore, not an immediate or accidental cause in particular cases. He under-lies the whole series. His causality is not occasional or accidental, but immanent. He works through the laws of nature, of *prakriti*; it is *prakriti* or *Swabhava* which evolves itself. But *prakriti* is by its nature *jada*; it has no life, no activity. Only an intelligent being can be a source of activity. There cannot be any motion on the part of bodies destitute of souls.[50] Pure intelligence indeed

---

49. S. B. II. 3. 41.   50. S. B. IV. 4. 15.

is not active; but it can move other objects as magnet moves iron. " So the Lord also who is all-present, the Self of all, all-knowing and all-powerful, although himself unmoving, moves the universe."[51]

Such a statement of the problem is far from being a full and adequate one. It leaves much to be accounted for. Shankara in fact saves to a great extent the law of causation and the ultimate agency of God. But plainly speaking, there is no place for freedom of will, for self-determination in this theory. Man is tied down helplessly to the series of events, to the operations of *Prakriti*. To invoke the eternity of *Samsara* is to take the problem back infinitely; it is not to explain it. And even then the freedom to act *here* and *now* —the most vital fact in our ethical life—is practically denied. Not only in his sufferings and happiness, but in all his actions, man is dependent upon his own previous deeds. The present comes helplessly out of the past and the

---

51. S. B. II. 2.2.

future from the present. Freedom of will is openly sacrificed at the altar of causality.

But all this is valid only in the empirical sphere. Here human actions are purely phenomena and the laws of time, space and causality ("कालदेशनिमित्त") governing all phenomena are paramount in the case of man's activities also. In the realm of *Brahman*, of pure spirit, man is free. All hindrances, all determinations disappear. But this freedom only means freedom from the categories of the understanding, of the restrictions of *Avidya*. It does not mean free activity, as we understand it, in our ethical discussions. Because activity is a feature only of the empirical existence, it therefore disappears along with its other features, as time, space, causality. The soul indeed is free (मुक्त); but this conception is negative, owing to the very limitations of our conceptual faculty and of our powers of expression. It is free only with reference to this empirical world of ours; but what in itself it is, no eye can see, no ear can hear, nor any heart can conceive.

Whatever may be the significance of the rôle of morality from the point of view of the Absolute, its significance in the realm of *Avidya* cannot be ignored. It must be said to the credit of the moral consciousness of the Hindus that far from explaining away morality as an accident in the evolution of society, it took it to be the very essence, the vere source of creation. In fact, the universe was conceived only as a theatre of good and bad deeds of creatures and consequently their happiness and unhappiness. Here जगत् is defined." It is differentiated by names and forms, contains many agents and enjoyers, is the abode of the fruits of actions, these fruits having their definite places, times and causes."[52] It is the *Karma* of a being which is responsible for its happiness and unhappiness, its transmigration into various forms of bodies. When evil tendencies predominate (" स्वाभाविकदोषबलीयस्त्वात् ") and a being indulges in evil deeds, it has to descend to

---
52. S. B. I. 1. 2.

lower forms of being than it occupied before. When higher tendencies reign supreme ("शास्त्रसंस्कारबलीयस्त्वात्") a being rises into higher worlds. When the two forces, evil and good, counterbalance each other, a being assumes the form of a human being. [53]

Every individual carries along with him in his journey of *Samsara* a *Karma-ashraya*, a moral substratum, which determines his character and destiny. In the *Brihadaranyaka Upanishad*, it is said that three factors accompany a soul : his knowledge, his actions and his previous experience. [54] This last factor takes the form of impressions left behind in the soul by the experiences of previous deeds. This *vasana* influences a man's new actions and the results of actions already done. It is impossible for a man either to start any action or to enjoy the fruit of any previous action without this factor. It is to its presence and its greater or less power that all the different degrees

---

53. Br. C. IV. 4. 6.   54. Br. IV. 4. 2.

of skill and talents in the different departments of life are due. 55

The previous deeds of a man's life accompany a man in the form of an *apurvam*. This principle is used by Jaimini : " It is clear that a deed cannot effect a result at some future time, unless before passing away, it gives birth to some unseen result ; we (therefore) assume that there exists some result which we call *apurva*, and which may be reviewed either as an imperceptible after-state of the deed or as an imperceptible antecedent state of the result. " 56 Shankara adopts this idea with this modification that in his theory this supersensuous principle cannot of itself give rise to any fruit, because it is unintelligent. 57 The agency of God is necessary to bring about the results of all deeds. 58

The next problem is the attitude of the liberated souls before they die ; and connected with this is the place of morality

---

55. Br. C. IV. 2;   56. S. B. III. 2. 39.
57. S. B. III. 2. 38.   58. S. B. III. 2. 40.

from the point of view of the Absolute. Here the *Vedanta* of Shankara maintains the strictly super-moral attitude. Morality is a factor of considerable value in one state of our existence, but it is necessarily transcended when we leave all empirical views and attain the beatific vision. The very distinction between the good and evil, between morality and immorality belongs to our limited point of view. Such is the super-moral attitude. A man, who has attained the absolute is, therefore, in a similar predicament. The law of *Karma* ceases to have any validity for him. He can do deeds but is not bound by their consequences. Because the power of *Karma* lies in " egotism and desire of rewards "; in our *Avidya*. " It is but right that actions should pollute those men of the world, who are attached to their actions, thinking themselves to be the authors thereof, and longing for the fruits of such actions; as I have none of these (viz. desire and attachment) actions cannot bind me. Any other person, too, who knows me to be his Self, who thinks 'I am no agent, I have no longing for the fruits of actions.'—his actions too will not necessitate incarnation."[59] Again, it follows that as soon as a man by virtue of his highest knowledge places himself above all laws of *prakriti*, his former sins also lose their force.[60] In the same way all good works are destroyed also. But the actions by which this body has been brought into existence, will come to an end only when their effects have been fully worked out; for those actions have already commenced their effects.[61] Such is the reason why the body of a liberated sage continues to exist even after he realizes the knowledge of *Brahman*.

The liberated sage enters the super-moral and super-religious stage of life. Neither moral nor religious injunctions have any validity for him. " It is our ornament and pride that as soon as we comprehend *Brah-*

---

59. Bg. C. IV. 14.   60. S. B. IV. 1. 13.
61. Bg. C. IV. 37. S. B. IV. I. 15.

man all our duties come to an end and all our work is over."⁶³ " Nor does it result from the absence of obligation, that he who has arrived at perfect knowledge can act as he likes, for in all cases it is only the wrong imagination (of the self's connection with the body) that impels the actions, and that imagination is absent in the case of him who has reached perfect knowledge."⁶³ " As to free action (यथाकामित्वं) as one likes it, it is quite unnatural in the case of a wise man; for we know it to be proper to one who is extremely ignorant. To explain : when even the action prescribed by the *Shastras* is regarded as a heavy burden and unnatural to one who knows the Self, how can wilful action caused by extreme thoughtlessness be ragarded as appropriate to him ? A thing seen under the effect of the deluded or diseased sight will certainly not remain the same even after the delusion or disease has disappeared; for it has its source in these alone. Thus it

---

62. S. B. I. 1. 4. ; Br. IV, 3. 22.
63. S. B. II. 3. 48.

is proved that he who knows the Self has no action incumbent on him, nor can he act at his own sweet will." [64]

The *Adwaita* of Shankara may be supposed to be fatal to the ethical life of humanity. Morality and immorality appear as mere illusions from the standpoint of the Absolute. Thus to a certain extent, it must be confessed that the ethical problems lose that fundamental importance which they possess for the ethical theisms of the West. The centre of gravity is shifted for the eastern sages from the kingdom of actions to the kingdom of thought and from the sphere of consciousness to the sphere of pure gnosis or superconsciousness. The few exalted spirits, who have kindled the immortal fire within themselves, raise themselves at a stroke from the empirical world with all its thought distinctions and moral appreciations to the transcendental world of pure spirit, where human judgments and provincial valuations of our planet

---

64. Ai. c. Introduction.

disappear ; and these again possess that absolute freedom, absolute happiness of which they can have only a glimpse here. The nearest (but very rough) approximations to such an ideal are the philosophers of Plato's Republic moving among pure, formless essences, in the kingdom of Ideas or Spencer's perfect men in perfect societies following the rules of Absolute Ethics or gods of Epicurus enjoying in perfect tranquillity the highest of pleasures.

In practical life, (Plato's world of shadows) the influence of the teaching of *Adwaitism* is of the purest and loftiest type. Moral life of humanity is deprived of one great support and supplied with another but more powerful one. The very foundation of our ordinary righteousness is taken away ; its egoistic basis disappears. This egoistic morality is necessarily narrow, provincial and sectarian; it sets individuals, against individuals communities against communities, nations against nations. It worships individual as the highest product of civilization. It over-emphasizes the importance of personal considerations. But Plato rightly divined that the ills of the world will not disappear till kings were philosophers or philosophers kings. (i. e. possessed of the vision of the Whole, seeing things fundamentally, and not taking the narrow, individual standpoint) The *Adwaitism* extends the idea one step further and lays it down that men must be philosophers and philosophers men and then will come the promised land, not flowing indeed with milk and honey but flowing with spiritual peace and harmony and happiness. The Self of an individual is the Self of the universe; and the conduct of every being must be regulated by what constitutes the good of the universe. This language is only a paraphrase of Kant's dictum: "Act in such a way that your conduct may be a law to all beings;" of Jesus Christ " Do towards others as you would wish them to do towards you;" of Plato, " The society must be ruled by the Idea of the Good, the happiness and greatness of the whole." There is no good of a part which is not a good of the whole. The *Vedanta* proposes to remove not only men's miseries, but the very roots of their miseries, not only their immorality but the seeds of their narrow virtues and narrow vices. Jesus Christ supplied the moral basis to this great ideal when he placed the essence of the Self in willing not in knowing; Gautama Buddha founded this ideal in the very heart of man, in his love, broad and disinterested for all life; Shankara representing the Hindu thought placed this ideal on its proper intellectual basis and thus secured a true philosophic foundation for the ideal of fundamental unity of mankind by boldly proclaiming that the individual Self is intrinsically the same as the soul of the universe.

CHAPTER VI

A COMPARISON OF SHANKARA'S SYSTEM WITH SOME MODERN PHILOSOPHIES.

THE IDEAL OF PHILOSOPHY: Two momentous facts confront us at the outset:— the one is flux, change, becoming; the other is the unchangeable, the imperishable. Now of these two, which is more fundamental? Some of the most radical differences in philosophy are due to the difference of emphasis on the one or the other of these two factors. Attempts are also made to reconcile these two. Some of these attempts were foredoomed to failure. A mechanical juxtaposition or an external unity between these two sides of nature is entirely useless. What is required is a philosophy which explains both sides of Reality, finds out their harmony and reconciles them in a deeper unity. Philosophy is largely a question of proportion. Any dogmatic, one-sided emphasis on one of these moments of Reality is suicidal. Comprehensiveness is the very essence of a great philosophical system; it must be capable of explaining all things from the great Absolute to a blade of grass. Such a system of philosophy must be both idealistic and realistic; for in it ideas and outer facts get due recognition and receive their proper place in a broader synthesis. It must be both monistic and pluralistic, for it does not sacrifice the one at the altar of the many, nor the many at the altar of the one; but in it both the one and the many become perfectly reconciled with each other. It must not be a brutal materialism, which worships facts and ignores values, idolizes science, and neglects religion and morality; nor must it be predominantly a philosophy of values, which goes on evading and ignoring all connection with facts and builds up for itself a magnificent 'Palace of Art', out of all possible reach for humanity. But it appreciates fully the significance of both facts and values and tries to explain intelligibly the relation of the one to the other. At the same time a great system of philosophy is something very remote from eclecticism, a mechanical union of these diverse elements, a superficial harmony of these fundamental discords, but a bold, original, characteristic structure of thought in which all elements find their appointed place, and get their meaning and significance in the light of the Whole.

Such is a brief outline of the ideal of unification towards which the philosophic world is steering. But it is an ideal only, and there is hardly any system of thought which satisfies all these conditions. This is only the extreme limit, the measuring rod, the standard by which all the existing philosophies may be judged. We shall now compare our philosopher's system with other systems of thought and thus by the light which the latter will throw upon the former, we will be able to elucidate more clearly some of the essential elements of its thought.

COMPARATIVE

SHANKARA AND MODERN IDEALISM.

The founder of modern idealism is Descartes. He deserves the credit of laying down the fundamental basis of all modern philosophy, in his celebrated proposition *cogito ergo sum*. 'I think, therefore I am'. With the enunciation of this proposition a great step was taken in philosophy. Self-consciousness was conceived for the first time to be the basis of all reality. Shankara in the East realised with equal clearness this cardinal fact of all idealism. " Just because it is the Self, it is not possible to doubt the Self. For one cannot establish the Self (by proof) in the case of any one, because in itself it is already known. For the Self is not demonstrated by proof of itself. The Self is the basis of the action of proving, and consequently it is evident before the action of proving. And since it is of this character, it is therefore impossible to deny it." Shankara therefore, in common with all modern idealists makes the Self the one supreme, ineradicable assumption, which makes all knowledge, all reality possible.

Another great step forward was taken by Berkeley. Berkeley's great merit consisted in the fact that he proved it convincingly for all time the absurdity of the conception of matter as an absolutely independent substance. He asks the very relevant question: "*What is meant by the term Exist when applied to sensible things?*"[1] And he answers: "*The absolute existence of unthinking things without any relation to their being perceived*, that is to me *perfectly unintelligible*. Their *essi* is *percipi*, nor is it conceivable that they should have any existence out of the minds of thinking things which perceive them."[2] And his proof is this: "It is but looking into your own thoughts, and so

---
1.–2. Selections from Berkeley. p. 34.

trying whether you can conceive it possible for a sound, or figure or motion, or colour to exist without the mind or unperceived... To make out this, *it is necessary that you conceive them existing unconceived or unthought of,* which is a manifest repugnancy." [3] Berkeley's position therefore comes to this: no object without a subject. This is the element of permanent truth in Berkeleanism. For Shankara also the refutation of materialism consists essentially in the imposibility of conceiving an absolute, independent existence of all material things. Shankara's position is this: Whatever can be the object for a subject is matter (or we may put it: Matter is that which can only exist as an object for a subject); whatever cannot be an object for a subject (that is whatever is eternally subject) is spirit. The former has, therefore, a secondary existence, dependent on the perceiving mind, the latter alone has an independent existence, an absolute reality, an

---

3. **Selections** from Berkeley p. 48-9.

existence not derivative, nor secondary but existence in itself. "Shapes cannot have their own shape or another as object, while on the other hand, consciousness has as object the elements and their products, whether without or within the Self. As the existence of elements and products is concluded from the fact that they are perceived, so that the conclusion must also be drawn that this perception is different from them (perception makes the material world known and not *vice versa*) and perception is just the proper nature of what we call soul."[4] In the commentary on the *Karikas* of Gaudapada and *Vivekachudamani*, Shankara argues that material existence is mind-dependent, because it is present when mind is present and absent (at the time of deep sleep). And it is equally clear to both Berkeley and Shankara that ideas also have no independent reality; they have reality so far as they belong to some person (or spirit as Berkeley puts it). Ideas according to Berkeley are

---

4. S B. III. 3, 54. tr. Dr. Deussen 269.

unthinking things.⁵ and the very *existence* of an unthinking thing consists in *being perceived*.⁶ The whole existence of reality is resolved by Berkeley into *spirits* and *ideas*. " The former are active, indivisible substances ; the latter are inert, fleeting or dependent beings, which subsist not by themselves, but are supported by or exist in, minds or spiritual substances."⁷ Shankara's view of the relation of ideas to soul, is the same as Berkeley's. " As the idea only is apprehended by the self which witnesses the idea (is conscious of the idea) there results no *regressus ad infinitum*. And the witnessing self and the idea are of an essentially different nature, and may therefore stand to each other in the relation of knowing subject and object known."⁸ And Berkeley's view of spirit and Shankara's view of soul, have much in common. For both, the

---

5. Selections from Berkeley. p. 91.
6. Selection from Berkeley. p. 93.
7. Selections from Berkeley. p. 94.
8. S. B. II. 2 28.

supreme reality consists in spirit or soul, for both, it is the sole source of activity, all intelligence; for both, it cannot be apprehended by means of an idea. " A spirit is one simple, undivided active being.—Hence there can be no idea formed of soul or spirit; for all ideas whatever being passive and inert cannot represent unto us by way of image or likeness, that which acts.... Such is the nature of spirit, or that which acts, that it cannot of itself be perceived, but only by the effects it produceth."[9] Shankara says : " it may be urged if *Atman* is ever incomprehensible, it may be something unreal. This cannot be, for we see its effects as plain as anything. As we infer the existence of the illusionist from effects such as the production of different forms etc. brought about by existent worker of the illusion, so visible effects such as the birth of worlds etc. must lead us to infer the existence of the absolutely real *Atman*, the substratum of the whole of illusion as spread out in the

---

[9]. Selections from Berkeley. p. 52.

variety of forms etc."[10] But differences between these two philosophers are also very great. Berkeley has left obscure in his system the relations between God and spirits. And he has invoked God's agency to establish the connectedness of the outer world. In fact, Berkeley's main contribution to philosophy lies in his refutation of the dogma of an object without a subject, of an independent and absolute existence of matter. And this kernel of his teaching became a part of all idealism; and as we have seen on this point, he is in fundamental agreement with Shankara also.

Hume showed the untenability of certain assumptions in Berkeley's system and showed a necessity for a deeper analysis. The transition from Berkeley and Hume to Kant is a very apt parallel to the philosophic movement from the sceptical position of *Bauddhas* to the idealist position of Shankara. Berkeley dissolved the world of matter into ideas of the human or divine

---

10. Karikas C. III. 27

brain. Hume finished the work of destruction by applying the same criticism to the idea of soul or spirit or substance. Matter as unrelated to subject does not exist; because we cannot form an intelligible idea of an independent material world. Well, says Hume, neither have we got an idea of spirit. All that we feel, is a series of impressions and ideas; the idea of the soul or substance behind them is as absolutely illusory, as the idea of a material substratum, an unknown somewhat which produces the sensations, in us. In this way, all our experience is resolved into a flux of sensations, a dance of ideas. The *Bauddhas* also denied the existence of outer world and also the existence of the soul. The *Vignanavadins* were subjective idealists, for whom the sole reality consisted in series of ideas which were self-conscious. Another point common with both these sceptical movements was that they took away the ordinary basis of causality and could not secure any other basis.

Shankara's position with regard to the *Bauddhas* very much resembles Kant's position with regard to Berkeley and Hume. In both these great philosophies the spirit of man becomes conscious of the necessity of a deeper analysis of experience owing to the difficulties revealed by scepticism. Both Shankara and Kant were convinced that scepticism (Shankara used to style it शून्य- वादप्रसंग.) was an impossible attitude of mind. Kant absorbed Berkeley's teaching so far as to deny the existence of the world of matter unrelated to all intelligence. Shankara similarly with the *Bauddhas* could not conceive of the outer or inner world of reality not dependent upon mind. But here they part company with the sceptical theory. Kant tries to preserve the empirical reality of the outer world against Berkeley. For Berkeley the outer world was dissolved absolutely into ideas; the object completely melts away into the subject. But Kant maintains that the inner life has no more meaning except with reference to an outer life. Berkeley points out that "for a sensitive subject such a world can exist only through its own affections, and therefore cannot be known to exist apart from them. The Kantian answer is that while for such a subject there would be no external world as such, neither would there be any consciousness of sensations as states of the self. The life of a purely sensitive being is not for it an *inner* life. i. e. not a consciousness of a series of states of its own being, any more than it is a consciousness of an outer world of objects. On the other hand, the self-conscious being which *has* an inner life cannot separate it from the outer life which it presupposes. Its inner life is not the consciousness of a series of sensations as such, but of perceptions or ideas which refer to external objects."[11] Here is Shankara's reply to the *Bauddhas*: "The nonexistence of external things cannot be maintained because we are conscious of external things. In every act of percep-

---

11, Caird ; Philosophy of Kant. Vol. I. 642.

tion we are conscious of the same external thing, corresponding to the idea whether it be a post or a wall or a piece of cloth or a jar, and that of which we are conscious cannot but exist.... That the outer world exists apart from consciousness has necessarily to be expected on the ground of the nature of consciousness itself. Nobody when preceiving a post or a wall is conscious of its perception only, but all men are conscious of the posts and walls and the like as objects of the perception."[12] Both Kant and Shankara base their refutation of sensationalism on a proper analysis of consciousness, which reveals that both our inner and outer states, both our subjective and objective feelings are conditioned by one another. In this sense mind is the correlate of matter, and matter the correlate of mind. " The inner and outer states, subjective and objective factors are related as cause and effect to one another." [13]

Further, while Hume had resolved the world of inner experience into a mere string

---

12. S. B. II. 2. 28.   13. Karikas C. 2, 16.

of unrelated ideas, Kant tries to reinstate the self to its original position by making it the fundamental condition of all experience. Empiricism states that knowledge is imprinted upon our minds from without. Mind is *tabula rasa*, experience is merely the object making itself felt on this white sheet. Berkeleian idealism invokes God to account for the possiblity of experience as an orderly system. But the role of self as a selective, active principle working spontaneously to make the subjective world of experience was dark to him. Hume worked on the premisses of empiricism; and hence his failure to account for order and unity in our experience. Kant took a wider and deeper view of human nature; he found that the cardinal feature of all experience is the idea of self. Ideas do not hang in the air; they are essentially personal. An idea unrelated to self, unappropriated by a personality can never be imagined to exist. "All the manifold determinations of perception must necessarily be related to the 'I think' in the subject that is conscious of it. The consciousness 'I think' cannot be given to the subject, but must proceed from the spontaneous activity of the subject. It is called *pure* apperception or pure self-consciousness, because it is the universal form which is necessarily presupposed in all modes of consciousness whatever. It is, therefore distinguished from empirical consciousness, inasmuch as the latter involves a particular relation to sense or feeling. It is also called *original* apperception, because it is the primary condition without which there can be no self-consciousness whatever, and therefore, no unity in our experience. And this ' I think ' is the only idea which occupies the position of being presupposed, explicitly or implicitly, in every form of consciousness."[14] Shankara similarly maintains that the self is absolutely necessary to render the ideas conscious. " If you maintain that the idea, lamplike, manifests itself withouts standing in need of a further principle to illuminate it, you main-

---

14. Watson; Philosophy of Kant explained. p. 146

tain thereby that ideas exist which are not apprehended by any of the means of knowledge, and which are without knowing being; which is no better than to assert that a thousand lamps burning inside some impenetrable mass of rocks manifest themselves...And if you finally object that we, when advancing the witnessing Self as self-proven merely express in other words the *Bauddha* tenet that the idea is self-manifested, we refute you by remarking that your ideas have the attributes of originating, passing away, being manifold and so on (while our self is one and permanent),- we thus have proved that an idea like lamp requires an ulterior intelligent principle to render it manifest."[15] "And further, when it is said that ' It is I, who know what at present exists, it is I, who knew the past, and what was before the past, it is I, who shall know the future and what is after the future,' it is implied by these words that even when the effect of knowledge alters, the

---

15. S. B. II. 2. 28,

knower does not alter, because he is in the past, future and present, for his essence is eternally present." Another point in which Kant and Shankara make a considerable advance upon their predecessors must be noticed. The latter failed to arrive at a right solution because in them the consciousness which was the object of analysis was some one individual consciousness. But Kant and Shankara widen the sphere of analysis when they make not this or that consciousness, but consciousness in general the object of their investigations. It is this which Shankara means by the distinction between अहंप्रत्ययविषय and अस्मत्प्रत्ययविषय (S. B. I. 1. I. 4. 4. II. 3. 38.) In the same way, Kant as well as Shankara vindicate the empirical validity of the law of causation. Kant accounts for it by making it a category of our understanding. But causality has no validity in the sphere of noumena. Shankara says: " It is *Jiwa* (individual soul conditioned by *upadhis*), whose very nature is bound up with the idea of cause and effect, as evidenced by such daily experience as ' I do this ' ' this happiness or that misery is mine ', and the like. *Atman* is absolutely free from any such idea, but in it is seen, like the snakes in place of the rope, the idea of *Jiwa*. Through it are evolved, by constituting the ideas of action, actor or act, as the ground of division, the various things, *prana* etc. subjective and objective. The cause of this ideation is thus explained. The self-evolved *Jiwa* having power to give shape to any idea, has its memory guided by its inherent knowledge. That is to say, from the knowledge of the idea of cause follows knowledge of the idea of effect; then follows the memory of the two; then again the knowledge and the variety of knowledge in the form of actor, act and actions. From knowledge arises memory and from memory knowledge, and this endless series continues without end, giving rise to various subjective and objective things." [16] Shankara has

---

16. Karikas, C. II. 16.

clearly grasped the fact, long before Hume, of the essentially subjective character of the category of causality. In the commentary on the *Sutras*, he expresses the same fact in a different way. " As the matter in hand is not one which can be known through inferential reasoning, our ordinary experience cannot be used to settle it. For the knowledge of that matter we rather depend on Scripture altogether, and hence Scripture only has to be appealed to." [17]

It is the distinction between phenomena and noumena in Kant's philosophy which brings it into real contact with Shankara's metaphysics. This distinction of the standpoints is fundamental in both these systems. Shankara distinguishes between *Vyavaharika* (realistic) and *parmarthic* (metaphysical) standpoints. Kant distinguishes between transcendental and empirical knowledge. Both are thus able to unite the empirical reality of the world with its transcendental ideality. All knowledge, says Kant, is only

---

17. S. B. I. 4. 27.

of phenomena; because all knowledge is essentially relative to our understanding. It is not the knowledge of the pure object as it is in itself, but the knowledge of the object as it is refracted through our senses and understanding. An element of relativity enters, therefore, into all our knowledge, and hence we do not know pure Reality, but Reality as it appears to us through the spectacles of our human senses and understanding. Hence our knowledge has not absolute validity, it has a comparative validity only. But then in the empirical realm, in the sphere of our existence as conditioned by our human limitations, all the categories of understanding are fully valid. But beyond these spheres, in the transcendental realm, these categories have no application. But how can we pass from phenomena to noumena, if we are enveloped everywhere by relativity? Here Kant brings his doctrine of practical reason; what is taken away as knowledge is restored as faith. Shankara virtually takes up an identical position. "The whole of experience i. e. duality made up of perceiver and perceived is pure imagination—a fiction of the mind which, in absolute truth is *Atman*, and is, as such not in relation with objects, eternal and absolute. The *Shruti* says : ' the *purusha* is always free from relation. ' That alone relates itself to objects which has any objects without itself; but the soul, having nothing external is perfectly free from all relation and therefore absolute."[18] " It may be asked what is the ground for saying that duality is a phenomenon of the mind, even like the imagination of a snake in place of rope. This is here shown on the strength of an inference ; and the conclusion to be established is this that ' All duality is of the mind ' in this sense. The reason for such conclusion is that it (duality) stands or falls with it (mind). When the mind is nought, when it is no mind, all its imaginings being withdrawn into itself like the snake in the rope, by the constant exercise

---

[18] Karikas C. IV. 72.

of discrimination and non-attachment, or even in sleep, duality is not experienced. Hence from an account of the absence of duality in experience, it follows that it does not exist."[19] The idea of ultimate Reality coincides in both the systems. "Kant's conception of thought is, that by its very nature whatever is positive—in other words what is real—must be real or complete in itself. From this point of view it is obvious that everything conceived to be real must be independent of all relation to anything else. If thought can only admit that which is self-complete to be real and exclude from this reality all contradiction, clearly reason will demand an individual which contains within itself all positive predicates to the exclusion of all relations and negations. This is what is meant by the Ideal of Pure Reason."[20] Gaudapada defines Reality as distinguished from appearance (Shankara expands this definition), "By the nature of a thing is understood that which is com-

---

[19] Karikas C. III, 31. [20] Watson 286.

plete in itself, that which is its very condition, that which is inborn, that which is not artificial or that which does not cease to be itself."[21] " Now that (is said to be) real, of which our consciousness never fails, and that to be unreal of which our consciousness fails."[22] Hence Shankara relegates all relative reality, all reality which has reference to our limited powers to the realm of *Maya*, because relativity which means change is incompatible with the absolute reality. All the universe of names and forms is therefore due to *Maya* ; in Kant's language it is a ' phenomenon '.

Shankara and Spinoza : A detailed consideration of the systems of a few philosophers will not be out of place here. Spinoza's system is an impressive attempt, like the Vedanta of Shankara, which captivates by its grandeur the human imagination. The initial impulse which led Spinoza to speculation was the same which prompted the movement of philosophic thought of the

---

21. Karikas. 22. Bg. C. II. 16.

Eastern sages.[23] It was spiritual rest Spinoza went after and his philosophy was directed to secure to him this satisfaction. There is no satisfaction in the finite and perishable things. This is the source of Spinoza's system. Therefore Spinoza thinks with Shankara that all unhappiness is due ultimately to ignorance, error, a false view of things. If ignorance is the root of all evil in the world, knowledge is salvation. The attainment of the right point of view as regards all existence is the one end of philosophy.

The method by which Spinoza proceeds is the same as Shankara's.[24] The existence of the Absolute is assumed rather than proved. It is the beginning of all inquiry not the end. " What Spinoza aimed at was a system of knowledge in which everything should follow by strict necessity of thought from the first principle with which it starts......It seeks to penetrate to the first ground or presupposition of all thought and being, to ' grasp that

---

23. Caird : Spinoza p. 9.   24. See Chapter I.

idea which represents the origin and sum of nature, and so to develop all our ideas from it that it shall appear as the source of all other ideas ' "[25] This is the very way in which Shankara proceeds, beginning like Spinoza, with *Brahman*, the Absolute, and deducing from it all the rest of the world.[26]

The Absolute was conceived by Spinoza as substance. It is " that which is in itself and is conceived through itself."[27] Like *Brahman*, it is the source of all explanation, but itself defies all explanation. Like *Brahman* it is co-extensive with reality; rather, it is itself the totality of existence. Like the idea of *Brahman* this idea cannot be proved, because all proof implies it.

Further, the substance of Spinoza has in itself no attributes.[28] It corresponds to the notion of *Nirguna* (pure) *Brahman*. *Brahman* has no attributes not at least the attributes which we conceive with regard to

---

25. Caird : Spinoza p. 113-4.
26. S. B. Introduction.   27. Caird ; Spinoza.
28. Caird : Spinoza. 136.

it. Yet *Brahman* becomes for us at once *Saguna Brahman*, and as such we predicate some attributes of it. The attributes of the substance are also not inherent in the substance; they are the differences which we ascribe to it. Thus the attributes of substance like the attributes of *Brahman* do not characterise the one or the other. They simply imply that Substance or *Brahman* appears to possess them, " in relation to the finite intelligence" which contemplates it. Another resemblance between the two systems is to be found in the fact that among the attributes predicated of God, two are emphasised as possessing special worth by both Shankara and Spinoza. These are "Thought and Extension" in the language of Spinoza; they are " Existence and Thought " in the words of Shankara. And these two really mean one and the same thing; substance is from one point of view Thought, and from another point of view Extension. Shankara would say that the very nature of *Brahman* is intelligence; and intelligence is not conceivable without existence.

The crux of both philosophies lies in the relation of the finite to the Infinite. Here also the movement of thought is the same in both cases. The Absolute in itself is pure, indeterminate, colourless unity. The very idea of an attribute, determination or difference in it, is fatal to its unity or reality. Reality is conceived as pure unity, pure identity, pure being. Shankara, therefore, resolves the fact of experience into two parts—the change and the changeless. The former he calls *Maya*, the latter reality. Spinoza comes to the same conclusion. We come to the idea of the Infinite by removing all the limitations which maked finite thing finite. His view is illustrated by the idea of space in us. This presents a close resemblance to Shankara's system, in which also the notions about *Brahman* are modelled upon those of *Akasha*—pure space. Space is one and continuous; and any division of it is purely fictitious. This conception is applied to all finite substances. The only reality which they possess is the reality of the Infinite Substance. Any individual reality which they possess is purely fictitious. Hence from the highest point of view, even God of theology becomes an illusion.[29]

But to say that the universe with all its variety and multiplicity of beings is mere illusion is not to explain it. There is another aspect of the question for us—the reality which we have got to ascribe to the world, if we are to live at all. An atmosphere of pure being is too ethereal for human imagination. When Spinoza and Shankara therefore descend from the pure heights of the Absolute to the particulars of our world, they allow a measure of reality to these things. Hence the movement in both cases from the idea of pure being, the undifferentiated unity which negates the reality of all time and space, of all individual distinctions, to the idea of a determinate Being, a *Saguna Brahman*, a qualified Absolute, which is the real ground of the whole universe, its centre

---

29. Caird : Spinoza. 143.

and its source. A negative Absolute (negative, of course from the point of view of the world) changes at once into a positive God. Man and nature, which were spirited away by the magic of a transcendental logic again appear and assume reality.

In the moral theory of Spinoza there are two points which resemble the corresponding ethical positions of Shankara. The first is the identification to a certain extent of intellect and will. The ultimate root of all evil is not wrong willing, but wrong knowing. Error or false view of the world is responsible for all sufferings. The second position is the absence of real freedom of will. The first stage of man is that of bondage. All finite things are conditioned and determined from without, and man among the rest. Eternal things act on man through the influence of the passions. 30 This corresponds to the idea of the *Vedanta* that man as a part of *Prakriti* is swayed hither and thither by the power of the

---

30. Caird : Spinoza p. 264.

three *Gunas*. But in Spinoza's system, man is free from the point of view of the highest intelligence, as in Shankara's system the *Atman* as such is free. The human ego by identifying itself with the universal essence becomes free.

The concept of causality receives almost identical treatment in either case. Here also there are two aspects of the problem. There is a sort of reality which we ascribe to this fact. This elementary concept we have to take for granted; it means an unconditional succession. Thus both Shankara and Spinoza say that God is the cause of the world. We have seen Shankara's position when he proceeds to prove how *Brahman* is the cause of the world. Spinoza also says : " God is the efficient cause of all things that can fall under an infinite intellect. " The modes of any given being have God for their cause.[31] But this elementary causal concept is soon replaced by the ideal causal concept. Ordinary cau-

---
31. Caird : Spinoza, p. 167.

sation is evidently a category of the finite. It implies the succession or co-existence of its members. In the former case, the cause loses itself partially or wholly in the effect. In the latter case we have to take things as external to and also affected by each other. Thought, therefore, works down from the elementary idea of causation to an ideal concept in which there is complete identity of cause and effect. [32] Like Shankara, therefore, Spinoza says " God is *omne esse* ". The relation between cause and effect is conceived ultimately as one of identity.

SHANKARA AND BERGSON.

A comparison of some philosophical positions of Shankara with those of Bergson is sure to be very instructive. Particularly because Bergson claims to emphasise just those aspects of experience which were relegated into background by Shankara, and neglects the importance of those which were fundamental for Shankara. Being is the one central fact in Shankara's philosophy; becom-

---

32. Hoffding : Problems of Philosophy. p. 98.

ing is the central word of Bergson's philosophy. Shankara's philosophy is a philosophy of the changeless; Bergson's system is a philosophy of change. The one denies the existence of time; to the other time is the very stuff of reality. Notwithstanding such abrupt contrasts in matters the most fundamental, Bergson's thought is, in some respects, a very useful commentary on Shankara's speculation.

What is the specific contribution of Bergson to philosophic thought? It lay in this. Philosophic speculation had come almost to a deadlock. Since the time of Descartes, many attempts were made to overcome the dualism of subject and object, mind and matter. Descartes posited the dualism and then tried to overcome it by bringing in God. Spinoza sees these two as mere parallel expressions of Substance. Berkeley also brings in the *tertium quid* of God. It was the same with Leibniz. Kant went much further. He said that understanding creates nature, that mind instead of being merely the passive recepient of impressions from the outside world, is itself the cause of the ordering of the world by means of its forms. Experience is twofold : matter and form. Mind imposes its form on matter. But what then, this matter ultimately is ? We know it so far as it is refracted through our understanding. Hence matter as it is in itself or as it is for a perfect understanding is something quite unknown and unknowable to us. It is the thing-in-itself—the noumenon. Thus the world was sundered into two parts—phenomena; and noumena ; the former are within the sphere of our knowledge, the latter are beyond it. This means that our knowledge is always relative and we are debarred for ever from knowing reality. It was a sorry pass to which philosophy was thus brought. Hence the system thus became an unconcious mainspring of all the latest agnostic systems. If reality is unknowable, we must take to either agnosticism or scepticism.

Bergson claims to deliver philosophy from

this *impasse*. We know that both Kant and Shankara think reality to be unknowable. Bergson agrees with this position. Intellect as it is, is incapable of comprehending reality. Shankara's position is explained in the next chapter. Bergson has brilliantly shown that intellect is essentially disqualified as an instrument of knowing reality. Why ? Because the very nature of reality is change. But intellect is characterized by a natural inability to comprehend life. [33] There is the brand of relativity on all our knowledge. There are two ways of knowing a thing: " The first implies that we move round the object; the second that we enter into it. The first depends on the point of view at which are placed and on the symbols by which we express ourselves. The second neither depends on a point of view, nor relies on any symbol. The first kind of knowledge may be said to stop at the relative; the second in those cases where it is possible,

---

33. Creative Evolution, 174.

to attain the *absolute*."34 Thus Bergson tries to solve the problem as to how it is possible for us to know the reality, the noumenon, the thing-in-itself or *Brahman*. His *absolute* knowledge is called *intuitive* knowledge, in which all duality, even of subject and object disappears. Analysis is laborious; intuition is a simple fact. This is the very point of Shankara's criticism of the uselessness of the study of *Shastras*, from the point of view of the Absolute. *Shastras* represent labour of thought, of intellect; they may merely mean multiplication of the points of view; hence there will be greater and greater conflict; and still we shall be outside the Absolute. Intuition alone can take us into the heart of the object; we therein become one with it; we catch its very spirit; we observe it from its very centre. As W. James says: " Reality, life, experience, concreteness, immediacy—use what words you will, exceeds our logic, overflows and surrounds it."35 Bergson,

---

34. An Introduction to Metaphysics. 1.
35. A Pluralistic Universe. 212.

therefore, introduced into philosophy, this novel point of view and worked it out very well. Shankara lays it down, like Bergson, that the true method of metaphysics is intuition; it is intuition alone which makes grasp of the Absolute, knowledge of the Reality possible. The very word *Darshana* applied to Hindu systems of philosophy points to the fact that it is ultimately sight or insight, intuition, immediate experience, direct realisation of the Absolute, they aim at.

There is some resemblance between two philosophers in other respects also. Shankara thinks that although the study of *Shastras* cannot bring us into touch with the Absolute, they can point the way to it; they can turn us away from irrelevant pursuits. Bergson also thinks that a preliminary preparation of this type is necessary. " For we do not obtain an intuition from reality, that is, an intellectual sympathy with the most intimate part of it—unless we have won its confidence by a long fellowship with its superficial manifestations."[36] Both Shankara and Bergson think that intuition is not radically different from perception. Shankara compares the two by saying that in both the object speaks and not the subject; and in both, therefore, error, hesitation, and diversity of views have not much scope. Bergson distinguishes between these two, calling perception, infra-intellectual, and intuition, supra-intellectual. Kant recognised only the former; hence his failure to reach the possiblity of experiencing the Absolute. Lastly, we may point out one more common feature. A single effort of intuition, says Bergson, is not sufficient. It must be systematically practised, it must be a habit, nay a very part of us. Shankara's emphasis on *manan* and *nididhyasa* point in the same direction. Both thinkers emphasize the extreme difficulty of the effort and lay down extensive study and much practice as the prerequisites of attaining it.

The above resemblances are rather obvious.

---

36. An Introduction to Metaphysics. 77--78.

But we can trace even in the other aspects of the philosophy, which seem to be at the very opposite pole to Shankara's system, a very subtle identity with the latter. *Brahman* is in many ways the same as Bergson's Reality. *Brahman*-it is true-is above time, the Reality as Bergson conceives it, is pure duration. But this is largely a difference of of phrase, and not of thought. Pure duration is entirely different from our ordinary notion of time, viz. a succession of states.[37] Bergson identifies duration with the sense of life and activity within us. This has nothing to do with our ordinary idea of time, which involves the distinction of the past, the present and the future. Thus practically Bergson approaches in his conception of pure duration the timeless Absolute of Shankara. Both are above all ordinary limitations of time; both are revealed by pure intuition; and both are at the centre of our free activity.

Bergson says that Reality is time, dura-

---

37. Wildon Carr : Bergson. 76.

tion, life, consciousness. It is cosmic *elan.* The cosmic life is the same as duration, the same as spirit. It is the Reality. It is the universal force operating everywhere. It is God. It is "incessant life, action, freedom." In man, as well as in nature, all force is this. Bergson, like Shankara does not believe in " The theory of the self as a separate individuality, radically distinct from other individualities human and divine. " *Brahman* is exactly like this original life-impetus, which is the one source of all life, activity, dynamics.

Thus Dr. Deussen defines *Brahman*: " Meanwhile.... the spiritual (*Chaitanyam*) is, in our system a potency which lies at the root of all motion and change in nature, which is therefore, for example ascribed to plants, and means rather the capacity of reaction to outer influences, a potency which in its highest development, reveals itself as human intellect, as spirit. " [38] The nature of this cosmic spirit, like the nature of

---

38. Dr. Deussen. p. 50.

Brahman is inscrutable to our intelligence. The ultimate force is in the last resort " something inexpressible, something incalculable, withstanding all analysis. "39 Both of these we can comprehend only by intuition, because *Brahman* or the life force is the very stuff of our individuality.

One of the interesting features of Bergson's philosophy is his account of matter. Matter is not something other than mind. It is the same life force which produces both. The essence of consciousness or life is freedom, creation, action, growth. Matter is nothing but the inversion of this movement, its interruption. It is the arrest of spirit. Extension or matter is the de-tension of tension. In our own individuality we observe that our consciousness goes on elaborating something new, but as soon as a thing becomes habitual and our attention ceases to accompany it, it becomes something material, some deposit of spirit. Matter is thus " a descending movement, a dispersion, a degradation of

---
39. J. M'killer Stewart. p. 88

energy, and life is in contrast an ascending movement."[40]

Thus neither the matter of Bergson, nor the Prakriti of Shankara is a positive, independent entity. The genesis of the matter is involved in the very nature of life or spirit. Therefore in either system, there is no dualism. The operation of the same spirit which accounts for life and consciousness, accounts for matter also. Further, in some of the great idealistic systems, intellect accounts for the world, but intellect itself remains unaccounted for. But Bergson, like Shankara traces the genesis of the intellect to the same source; Shankara traces it to Maya or prakriti; Bergson says that intellect is the deposit of spirit on its march. In both theories intellect is a negation of reality, hence its particular sphere is matter or Maya, which is also the negation of reality. There is an ontological affinity between matter and intellect, as there is an ontological affinity between life or spirit or

---

40. Wildon Carr. p. 86.

consciousness or duration or *Brahman* and intuition (which is in fact life itself).

CHAPTER. VII.

HOW FAR IS SHANKARA'S SYSTEM A PHILOSOPHY IN THE MODERN SENSE OF THE TERM ?
1. WHAT IS PHILOSOPHY ?

Philosophy is a very vague term and has apparently undergone considerable variation in meaning. But all the same, a certain unity of content is clearly discernible beneath these variations. The following implications appear to be common in all philosophies. (1) " Totality : philosophy is conceived as a comprehensive view, as dealing (objectively) with the whole or universe, and accordingly as (subjectively) requiring to be pursued in a catholic or impartial spirit. It is thus marked off from the special sciences which limit their view to some specific set of facts... (2) Generality : just because the view is a whole, it manifests itself in universals, in principles. (3) Application... The general truths do not remain inert or sterile, but are carried over to illuminate and make reasonable the relevant details."[1] Philosophy expresses a certain attitude, purpose, and temper of conjoined intellect and will, rather than a discipline whose exact boundaries and contents can be neatly marked off.[2]

With ourselves, philosophy has begun to acquire a definite meaning. The name does not stand any longer for all knowledge, human and divine. Encyclopœdic knowledge is now an impossibility. Nor will it be possible now to confound the provinces of theology and philosophy. The scholastic philosophy was rather a theology than a philosophy, it was absolutely dependent for its data upon outside authority. Modern philosophy takes its characteristic colour from the fact that it was a protest against the subordination of reason to any outside agency whatever. Its main note is freedom, freedom from the weight of authority in all its shapes and forms. Hence no system

---
1-2. Prof. Dewey : Philosophy (Baldwin's Dictionary of Philosophy).

will be entitled to the name of philosophy, in the modern sense of the term, which takes for granted a series of dogmas and incorporates these bodily into its organism. Such was the case with the philosophy of the middle ages and also of the jews. Hence these systems were rather theologies than philosophies. Theology may be dogmatic; revelation may be to it a sufficient justification for certain dogmas. But philosophy is bound to be critical; it is reason to which it ultimately appeals. None of the ingenious structures of men like Thomas Aquinas can stand this test; they are not, therefore philosophies in the present day use of the term. The Jewish philosophy was also nothing but an attempt to reconcile the teachings of Judaism with the results of secular sciences. It is therefore better to characterise the systems of these thinkers as theologies rather than philosophies. A point of some importance is the attitude of the modern mind towards the respective provinces of philosophy and sciences. Men like Herbert Spencer define philosophy as the sum of the results of sciences. Every science reaches certain conclusions; these are based upon some fundamental principles. Now a science of these ultimate principles will be an attempt towards unifying these generalisations by means of some ultimate law. This work of unification will be the province of a philosopher. But Spencer is not consistent in his account; he posits the Unknowable and makes it the object of thelogy. Whatever this may be, it is certainly not a Philosophy, which is after all an attempt to seek unity; and to sunder science and theology in this way is to give up even the possibility of uniting them. Philosophy cannot then afford to be merely a science of sciences or an appendix to sciences. It is not the results, but the presuppositions of sciences, the assumptions of our everyday life and the assumptions of our various sciences, which philosophy takes upon itself to consider. Sciences take portions of reality for study, but a study of all the parts is not the same thing as the study of the whole. The whole has a character of its own; it is not a sum of the characters of the parts. The universe is one fact, not a series of facts, and it is this fact which the philosopher has to consider. Philosophy, therefore, tries to take a systematic view of the whole, it asks questions about the ultimate things, the last and most general features of Reality. The whole may be attacked from the point of view of the subject or the object, or God; according as the one or the other is emphasized, philosophy becomes predominantly an epistemology (as with Kant—a theory of experience) or a cosmology (as with the Greek philosophers; a theory of the world) or a theology (as with the medieval philosophers). But it is always an independent investigation into the character of Reality taken as a Unit, as an organized whole, as a totality.

The latest phase of speculation in the West tends to bring out the importance of values along with facts. Prof. Sidgwick defines the final and most important task of philosophy as the problem of "connecting fact and ideal in some rational and satisfactory manner."3 Hoffding puts it thus: "the problem of philosophy is to find out the relation between what seems to us men the highest value and existence as a whole."4 Windelband says: " We do not so much expect from philosophy what it was formerly supposed to give a theoretic scheme of the world, a synthesis of the results of the separate sciences, or transcending them on lines of its own, a scheme harmoneously complete in itself; what we expect from philosophy to-day is reflexion on those permanent values which have their foundation in a higher spiritual reality above the changing interests of the times." 5 This view comes very near to the view of the office of philosophy of the Hindu philosophers, as we have pointed out in the introductory chapter. Philosophy gives up, therefore the hopeless task of co-ordinating

---

3. H. Sidgwick: Philosophy, its Scope and Relations. p. 30

4-5. Quoted: Idea of God. (A. Seth) 39.

the results of various sciences; it inquires into the meaning and value of our deepest and most fundamental beliefs about ourselves, God and the world and their mutual relations. It differs from theology in this respect, that it is reason to which it addresses itself and not authority. It differs from sciences inasmuch as it deals not with a portion of Reality, but the whole of it. It is, however scientific, as it is a reasoned system; it is thus distinguished from all traditional, haphazard or authoritative beliefs, but it is not a science among other sciences.

The question with regard to the place of Shankara in the history of philosophy is simply this: Is Shankara a mere theologian or a philosopher in the scholastic sense of the term? The answer to this question requires a detailed investigation into the epistemology of Shankara.

II. SHANKARA'S POSITION CONSIDERED WITH REFERENCE TO STATEMENTS IN HIS WRITINGS.

How do we account for the fact of knowledge? What are its sources? And what is its validity? How can we distinguish between truth and error? These are some of the vital questions which every philosopher has to answer. It is true that the consciousness of the limitations of our knowledge is a late growth in philosophy. The earliest philosophies were pure inquiries into the objective reality. Dr. Deussen points out that the " Indian philosophy did not start, as for the most part, the Grecian did, from an investigation free of assumptions into ' the existent ', but rather like modern philosophy from the critical analysis and testing of a complex of knowledge handed down (through the *Veda*)."[6]

The criteria of truth are known in the Hindu thought as *pramanas* or canons of knowledge. Shankara as well as other Hindu philosophers recognise in perception the one great source of knowledge. This was known as *pratyaksha* or the sensuously perceptible; that knowledge

---

6. Dr. Deussen. 82.

in which we come in direct contact with reality. A contact of the sense with the object produces the necessary conviction. It is realised that it is the main source of knowledge for the human beings and the sole source for animals. Perception takes place inevitaly and is not in the least dependent upon our will. It has a measure of reality which can never be taken away. We cannot accept the words of him who while perceiving a thing through his sense still says that he does not perceive the outward thing and that no such thing exists.[7] Another source of knowledge is *anumān* (inference). Inference either takes place from a cause to an effect or *vice versa*; or it takes place from one object to another analogous to it. It is based upon perception and derives its validity partly at least from it.

Shankara recognises other tests of truth also; such as, consistency or freedom from contradictions, the testimony of commn-sense, the authority of recognized men. He fre-

---

7. S. B. II. 2. 28.

quently rejects many theories, on the ground of the presence of discrepancies therein. He says : " Other views are refuted on the ground that they are full of contradictions. On the same ground the untenability of the Vedanta view may be exposed. Hence an attempt is made to clear off these "[8] In fact, he is throughout his writings trying to establish the connectedness of the conflicting passages of the Shrutis. Similarly, he recognizes the validity in a sense of the commonsense view of the world. Thus he argues against the subjective idealists that " Nobody feels that when he perceives the pillar or an outward object that he perceives the perception not the object. "[9] Again, " You refuse to recognize the common and altogether rational opinion that we are conscious of the external thing by means of the idea different from the thing. Indeed a proof of extraordinary insight. "[10] Authority of great people is not indeed entitled

---

8. S. B. II. 3. 1. 9. S. B. II. 2. 28.
10. S. B. II. 2. 28.

to much weight, because sometimes great men contradict each other.[11] Still authority has some title to belief. Shankara says that atomism is entirely unacceptable because no person of weight has accepted it.[12] Further, Shankara accepts the pragmatic test of truth. A statement of theory is true in proportion as it works successfully in practice. Truth is thus to be judged by its consequences, by the difference it makes to us when we accept it or reject it. Many positions are attacked on the ground that they would lead to the unsettling of the minds of the people. (लोकव्यवहारोच्छेदप्रसंगः) This is the argument advanced against the vague and confused reasoning of the Jainas and against the Bauddhas. Shankara argues that if the doctrine of momentariness be accepted the consequence will be the weakening of the people's faith in the doctrine of causality and consequent chaos. Similarly, all reasonings or theories which render the attainment of salvation improbable or impossible are to

---

11. S. B. II. 1. 11.   12. S. B. II. 2. 17.

be rejected. (अनिर्मोक्षप्रसंगः) The fundamental motive of philosophy of the Hindus is practical; it is the deliverance from all finite states.[13] The following sentences are almost pragmatic in their ring. It is said that he who accepts the right meaning of sentences either gets some positive good or at least can avoid some evil. Hence we can see that particular conclusions are correct or truthful, when we know that they lead to the attainment of good things; and judge that they are wrong when they lead to evil results. He who takes wrong things as right, a man as pillar, foe as friend, suffers.[14] Here truth is identified with good and error with evil. The whole Vedanta view in fact had its origin in procuring for man, freedom from the finite world, and hence any view which differred fundamentally from this position, was *ipso facto* erroneous.

Reasoning plays a rôle of no mean character in deciding the questions of truth and error

---

13. S. B. I. 4. 23.   14. Br. C. I. 3. 1.

in Shankara's system. In a passage put into the mouth of the opponent, Shankara points out the importance of reasoning as an organ of truth. It may be summarized thus :

(1) Reasoning is not only a principle of difference, but a principle of agreement also. (2) We must have a healthy confidence in our reaon, otherwise there shall be chaos. All human activity is based upon certain conclusions; and if all faith is shaken in the powers of our mind, society will collapse. (3) Even if it is meant to say that there is any higher source of truth, the fact that it is a higher source must be justified at the bar of reason. Hence reason in this case too becomes an ultimate arbiter. (4) Revelation requires the assistance of our reasoning power in elucidating its meaning, harmonising its teachings and so on. (5) Because some theories established by reasoning are false, it does not follow that all are and will be false.[15]

There are a few passages in which Shankara

---
15. S. B. II. I. 11.

says that reasoning alone is adequate to establish the foundation of his system.

"It is asked whether the Adwaita is to be taken as proved only on the evidence of the Shruti, and whether no reason can possibly demonstrate it. This chapter therefore shows how the Adwaita can be demonstrated by reason." "Duality has been shown to be mere illusion in the preceding chapter, by illustrations of dream, illusion, castle-in-the-air etc., and also by reasoning based on grounds such as the capability of being seen."[17]

Again, at the opening of the second chapter of the Mandukya, Shankara says:

"It has been already said, knowledge (gnosis) having arisen, duality does not exist, and this has been borne out by the Shrutis such as 'the unit is ever one' etc. This however is established on the authority of the word of holy writ. But it is possible also to show the unsubstantiality of the ob-

---
16. Ma. C. III. 1.
17. Ma. C III. 1,

jective from pure reasoning, and this second chapter is undertaken for that purpose."[18] " This Adwaita philosophy is the true one, because it has the support of the Shruti as well as reason ; every other system must be imperfect having no such authority."[19]

Revelation and reason are often considered two indispensable factors for the establishment of the Adwaita.

" The Madhu Kanda was based primarily on the authority of the Shruti; the Yagnavalkiya Kanda is based on reasoning, hence the knowledge of the self is arrived by both the scriptures and the reasoning....The conclusions based on both Revelation and Reason become completely reliable, because no objection can be taken to them."[20] " Now we are going to refute the arguments (of the Sankhyas) in an independent manner without any reference to the Vedanta-texts."[21] As a subsidiary factor, the value of reason-

---

18. Ma. C. II. 1.
19. Ma. C. III. 17.
20. Br. V. Introduction.
21. S. B. II. 2. 1.

ing is very often recognised; " while however the Vedanta passages primarily declare the cause of the origin &c. of the world, inference also being an instrument of right knowledge, is not to be excluded as a means of confirming the meaning ascertained. Scripture itself, however, allows argumentation."[22] "And if it has been maintained above that the scriptural passage enjoining thought (on *Brahman*) in addition to mere hearing (of sacred texts treating of *Brahman*) shows that reasoning also is to be allowed its place, we reply that the passage must not be deceitfully taken as enjoining bare independent ratiocination but must be understood to represent reasoning as a subordinate auxiliary of the holy tradition."[23] " Our final position, therefore, is that on the ground of scripture and of reasoning subordinate to scripture, the intelligent *Brahman* is to be considered the cause and substance of the world."[24]

---

22. S. B. I. 2.
23. S. B. II. 1. 6.
24. S. B. II. 1. 11.

Very important indeed is the contribution made by reason towards obtaining a satisfactory, ultimate view of the Reality. But Shankara very clearly perceives that an independent exercise of our dialectical faculties cannot take us into the heart of the Absolute. In a brilliant passage, he exposes the limitations of intelligence (or conceptual view of things) as the organ of the knowledge of *Brahman*.

" The true nature of the cause of the world on which final emancipation depends cannot, on account of its excessive abstruseness, even be thought of without the help of the holy texts; for it cannot be object of perception because it does not possess qualities such as form and the like, and as it is devoid of characteristic signs, it does not lend itself to inference and the other means of right knowledge. Perfect knowledge has the characteristic mark of uniformity, because it depends on actually existing things, for whatever thing is permanently of one and the same nature is acknowledged to be true or real thing, and knowledge conversant about such is called perfect knowledge, as for instance, knowledge embodied in the proposition ' fire is hot '. Now it is clear that in the case of perfect knowledge a mutual conflict of men's opinions is impossible. But that conclusions founded on reasoning do not conflict is generally known: for we continually observe that what one logician endeavours to establish as perfect knowledge is demolished by another, who in his turn, is treated alike by the third. Nor can we collect at a given moment and on a given spot all the logicians of the past, present and future time, so as to settle (by their agreement) that their opinion regarding some uniform object is to be considered perfect knowledge."[25]

Other passages also elucidate the same point.

" As *Brahman* is not an object of the senses, it has no connection with those other means of right knowledge. If *Brahman*

---

25. S. B. II. 1. 11.

were an object of the sense, we might perceive that the world is connected with *Brahman* as its effect; but as the effect only is perceived, it is impossible to decide (through perception etc.) whether it is connected with *Brahman* or something else. Therefore the Sutra under discussion is not meant to propound inference (as the means of knowing *Brahman*) but rather to set forth a Vedanta-text."[26] " It has indeed been maintained by the purvapakshin that the other means of proof also (and not merely sacred tradition) apply to *Brahman* on account of its being an accomplished entity (not something to be accomplished as religious duties are), but such an assertion is entirely gratuitous. For *Brahman*, as being devoid of form and so on, cannot become an object of perception; and there are in its case no characteristic marks (on which conclusions etc might be based), inference also and the other means of proof do not apply to it; but...it is to be known

---

26. S. B. I. 1. 2.

solely on the ground of holy tradition."[27]

In the commentary on Brihadaranyaka, Shankara repudiates the position of sophisters or pure reasoners.

" The rationalists who do not believe in the scripture, have rendered the meaning of the Shastras very uncertain, by applying contradictiry reasonings to the *Brahman* maintaining that ' it is ' and ' it is not ', ' it is active ' and ' it is not active '. Hence it is not possible to arrive at definite meanings in this way. But those modest followers who follow the holy traditions absolutely can as easily realise the subject of God etc., as they realise the objects of perception."[28]

" It is further argued that *Atman* is अप्रमेय (above all proofs) on the ground that the conception of प्रमेयत्व requires two things—the measure and the measured. But *Atman* is one, hence it is not capable of being judged by ordinary criteria of truth."[29]

---

27. S. B. II. 1. 7.
28. Br. C. I. 4. 6.
29. Br. C. IV. 4. 20.

On grounds such as these it is established that dialectic cannt grasp within its net the all-elusive Absolute.

The Vedas are claimed to be our only authority in matters of such fundamental importance as *Atman*, *Brahman* and the like. "Through Scripture only as a means of knowledge *Brahman* is known to be the cause of the origin etc., of the world."[30] The higher authority of the Shruties is vindicated on various grounds.

(I) They are an emanation from *Brahman* itself; they have been breathed forth by *Brahman*. "*Brahman* is the source i. e. the cause of the great body of Scripture, consisting of the Rig-Veda and other branches, which is supported by various disciplines; which lamp-like illuminates all things, which is itself all-knowing as it were. For the origin of a body of scriptures possessing the quality of omniscience cannot be sought elsewhere but in omniscience itself."[31] Elsewhere they are called अपौरु-

---

30. S. B. I. 1. 3.   31. S. B. I. 1. 3.

येय (of superhuman origin).³²

(2) The Vedas are eternal. "The eternity of the word of the Vedas has to be assumed for this very reason, that the world with its definite eternal species, such as gods and so on originates from it."³³ Just as the world of things was copied from the Platonic world of Ideas (in the system of Plato), so also according to Shankara all distinctions of all the different classes and conditions of gods, animals and men were regulated according to the species mentioned in the Vedas.

(3) The Shrutis were possessed of special authority because they were based on direct perception of the ancient Rishis (seers). Even Itihases and Puranas were considered as based on perception. " For what is not accessible to our perception may have been within the range of the perception of people in ancient times. Smritis also declare that Vyasa and others conversed with the gods face to face. A person maintaining that the

---

32. S. B. I. 2. 2.   33. S. B. I. 3. 29.

people of ancient times were no more able to converse with the gods than people are at present, would thereby deny the incontestable variety of the world. He might as well maintain that because there is at present no prince ruling our the whole earth, there were no such princes ruling over the whole earth in former times."[34]

(4) "The authoritativeness of the Veda with regard to the matters stated by it, is an independent and direct means of our knowledge; the authoritativeness of human dicta, on the other hand, is of an altogether different kind, as it depends on an extraneous basis (viz. the Veda) and is mediated by a chain of teachers and tradition."[35]

(5) " Release is only obtained from perfect knowledge. Perfect knowledge has the characteristic mark of uniformity, for whatever thing is permanently of one and the same nature is acknowledged to be a true and real thing, and knowledge conversant about such is called perfect knowledge.

---

34. S. B. I. 3. 133.   35. S. B. II. 1. 2.

Now it is clear that in the case of perfect knowledge a mutual conflict of men's opinions is impossible."[36] "The Veda which is the eternal source of knowledge, may be allowed to have for its object firmly established things, and hence the perfection of that knowledge which is founded on the Veda cannot be denied by any logician of the past, present or future."[37] Similarly it is said that while *Brahman* is one, the knowledge of it should be one also.[38]

(6) Mere reasoning cannot fathom the depths of the knowledge of such metaphysical realities as God and soul. " It is impossible to guess even the real nature of such a transcendental object as *Brahman* upon which depends liberation without the help of the holy tradition."[39] " For *Brahman* which rests exclusively on the holy texts, and regarding which the holy texts alone are authoritative–not the senses and so on,

---

36. S. B. II. 1. 11.   37. S. B. II. 1. 11.
38. S. B. III. 3. 1.   39. S. B. II. 1. 11.

must be accepted such as the texts proclaim it to be...Even certain ordinary things such as gems, herbs and the like possess powers which owing to difference of time, place and occasion, and so on, produce various opposite effects and nobody unaided by instruction is able to find out by mere reflexion the number of these powers, their favouring condition, their objects, their purposes etc., how much more impossible is it to conceive without the aid of scripture the true nature of *Brahman* with its powers unfathomable by thought."[40]

(7) The Shrutis are our only source of knowledge regarding transcendental things. All access to the noumenal reality being denied to perception and reasoning, we have necessarily recourse to the Shrutis. "Do not apply reasoning to what is unthinkable. The mark of unthinkable is that it is above all material causes. Therefore the cognition of what is supersensuous is based on the holy texts only."[41] " Nor can we assume

---
40. S. B. II. 1. 27.   41. S. B. II. 1. 27.

that some perceptions are able to perceive supersensuous matter without Shruti, as there exists no efficient cause for such perception."42 "Scriptural statement is our (only) authority in the origination of the knowledge of supersensuous things."43 " Such a transcendental reality is not the object of perception etc., it can only be cognised by the texts of the Vedas."44

Shankara's metaphysics has two aspects— the esoteric and exoteric. In the esoteric metaphysics or the pure philosophy of the Absolute, the quest of a criterion becomes impossible. In this respect Shankara's position resembles the position of Aristotle. Truth is one, absolute; hence there are no degrees of truth, there are degrees of error only.45 But the position is different from the point of view of ordinary experience. Shankara recognised that the nature and the validity of the tests of truth depend upon

---
42. S. B. II. 1. 1.
43. S. B. II. 3. II. 3. 1. 44. Br. C. I. 3. 1.
45. Prof. Ranade: Indian Philosophical Review

the appropriateness of the spheres in which they are employed. Thus we cannot assert offhand that one criterion is superior to another absolutely; in fact, there is no criterion of truth; there are criteria of truth. Shankara has grasped a very important truth inasmuch as he perceives the failure of the quest after one ultimate, absolute and all-comprehensive test, by the application of which it may be quite easy to draw off the exact line of demarkation between truth and error. From the point of view of action, those Shrutis which prescribe moral injunctions or prohibitions, acquire special validity, but if we adopt the standpoint of philosophy, the parts of Shruti which describe the ultimate unity acquire special weight. Therefore, the Vedanta which teaches the unity of *Brahman* does not stultify the ordinary Shastra; nor will the science of conduct be rendered useless. Nor does the science of conduct with its division of the agent etc. refute the authority of the Upanishads with their doctrine of the Unity of *Brah-*

num.⁴⁶ In the same way, the Shrutis can never shake our faith in the evidence of our senses. "The Shrutis are not authoritative with regard to the objects of other criteria. Thus we cannot say that fire is cold on any authority."⁴⁷ "It is not possible to maintain by means of a hundred instances that fire is cold or that the sun does not give light. Because reality will be known by other sources of knowledge. No one source of knowledge is contradicted by another source of knowledge. Every source of knowledge reveals the truth which is not the province of some other sphere of knowledge.". Thus Shankara comes to the conclusion that " स्वविषयशूराणि प्रमाणानि श्रोत्रादिवत् "⁴⁸. The sources of knowledge are only operative within their respective provinces. The application of a criterion must be justified by the appropriateness of its sphere. If, however, we cannot attack the sphere of senses in the name of Shrutis, neither can we bring in observation to refute

---

46. Br. C. III. 3. Intr.
47. Br. C. II. 1. 2.   48 Br. C. II. 1. 20.

the sense of the Shrutis. Neither observation nor reasoning are of any avail in a matter pertaining to the Shrutis. To the objection that intelligent agency belongs to efficient cause as in the case of potters and not to material causes, Shankara replies that " as the matter in hand is not one which can be known through inferential reasoning, ordinary experience cannot be used to settle it. For the knowledge of that matter we rather depend on scripture altogether and hence scripture only has to be appealed to. And that scripture teaches that the Lord who reflects before the creation is at the same time the material cause of it. "[19] This position can be taken up by the Vedantin, because he believes in the authority of the Shrutis, but not by those who do not believe in revelation. " The adherent of *Brahman* moreover, defines the nature of the cause, and so on, on the basis of scripture and is therefore not obliged to render his tenets throughtout conformable to observation. Our

---
19. S B. I. 4. 27.

adversary on the other hand, who defines the nature of the cause and the like, according to instances furnished by experience, may be expected to maintain only such doctrines as agree with experience."⁵⁰

To the above contention that the Vedanta need not consult experience as regards the causality of the world, an objection is raised, based on reasoning. " Although Scripture is authoritative with regard to its own special subject matter (as for instance, the causality of *Brahman*), still it may have to be taken in a secondary sense in those cases where the subject matter is taken out of its grasp by other means of right knowledge...Analogously, reasoning is to be considered invalid outside its own sphere; as for instance, in the case of religious duty and its opposite...The doctrine of *Brahman's* causality must therefore be abandoned as it would lead to the sublation of the well-established distinction of enjoyers and objects of enjoyment." ⁵¹ To this it is replied that

---
50 S. B. II. 2. 38.   51. S. B. II. 1, 13.

" Even on our philosophic view, the distinction may exist as ordinary experience furnishes us with anaogous instances. We see, for instance, that waves, foams, bubbles, and other modifications of the sea, although they really are not different from the sea-water, exist, sometimes in the state of mutual separation, sometimes in the state of conjunction."[52]

The special nature of the subject matter of metaphysics proper compels us to have recourse to some extra-ordinary organ of cognition, other than those means of knowledge usually employed in every-day life or in scientific investigation. All ordinary methods of knowing must necessarily break down when we want to conceive the inconceivable, to know the unknowable. Atman or *Brahman* is the goal of our investigation here. Now Atman cannot be grasped by senses. It cannot be an object of perception, because there is a conflict of views regarding Atman. [53]

---

52. S. B. II. 1. 13.
53. Br. C. I. Introduction.

It cannot be an object of inference, because there are no special marks or attributes by which we can infer its presence or nature.[54] Nor can it be an object of any Pramana, because it is Aprameya; it is one; and hence "केन कं विजानीयात्". It cannot be an object of knowledge, because knowledge implies duality of subject and object; there is the knower, the known and knowledge. But all reality is one, hence such distinctions (as ज्ञातृ, ज्ञान, ज्ञेय) cannot exist in the kingdom of the Absolute. In fact, all speech, all reasoning absolutely fail to make us aware of the nature of the Absolute. Even the Shrutis cannot therefore be the source of the knowledge of *Brahman*. If it should be objected that *Brahman* is not an object (of speech, mind etc.), the Shastras cannot possibly be its source, we refute this objection by the remark that the aim of the Shastras is to discard all disttinctions created by nescience. The Shastra's purport is not to represent *Brahman* as definitely

---

54. Br. C. II. 1. 20.

this or that object, its purpose is rather to show that *Brahman* as the eternal subject is never an object, and thereby to remove the distinction of objects known, knowers, acts of knowledge etc. which is fictitiously created by nescience. 55 The Shrutis do not introduce us into the positive nature of *Brahman*, they can only remove our illusions regarding it. They have the purport of diverting (men) from the objects of natural activity. For when a man acts intent on external things, only anxious to attain the objects of his desire and to eschew the objects of his aversion and does not thereby reach the highest aim of man although desirous of attaining it; such texts as the one quoted divert him from the object of his natural activity and turn the stream of his thoughts on the inward (highest) Self. 56 The function of the Shrutis, is, therefore a negative one; they destroy the obstacles on the road and the point the way to it.

---

55. S. B. I. 1. 4. 56. S. B. I. 1. 4.

They have no validity from the point of view of the Absolute. "The study of Shastras is useless when the Absolute is not known; and it is useless when the Absolute is realised." Revelation, too, therefore, labours to a certain extent under the same limitations as reason. It has to communicate itself in words; but no words can adequately describe the supreme Reality. Even the negative attributes used by the Shrutis with regard to the nature of *Brahman* are frail attempts to convey some notions of the Absolute: but these do not express with any degree of adequacy the existence and nature of *Brahman*. " That which cannot be grasped in words, which cannot be expressed, cannot possibly be analysed into this or that, having this or that attribute, permanent or impermanent...That the abstract Adwaita-thought should appear as describable in words, is only a feat of the mind, and nothing real."[57] It is stated that such epithets as अज (unborn) as applied to Atman

---
57. Má, C. VI.

are as much an outcome of illusion, as 'born'. " It is unborn only through such imagination as teaching and the like: in absolute reality it is not even unborn."[58] Shankara unhesitatingly declares that all means of knowledge and all scriptures (dealing with liberation as well as those devoted to injunctions and prohibitions) are based upon an illusion.[59] " The soul is the terminus of all organs of knowledge. When the knowledge of the true nature of the Self has been attained, neither organs of knowledge nor objects of of knowledge present themselves to consciousness any longer. The final authority (Veda) teaches that the Self is in reality no percepient of objects, and while so denying (i. e. as a result of that teaching), the Veda itself ceases to be authority, just as a dream perception (cease to be an authority) in a waking state "[60]

If the very nature of the supreme Reality disqualifies us from peeping into it by means

---

58. Ma. C. IV. 74.
59. S. B. I. 1. 1.   60. Bg. C. II. 69.

of either Shruti or reasoning, how are we to know the existence of such a thing as Atman or *Brahman*? *Brahman* will then become an impossible conception. The only tenable theory of metaphysics will then be agnosticism or perhaps scepticism. But Shankara does not want to take us into such an absurd situation. Reality is not abracadabra, a figment of an idle brain. It is not only knowable but knowable in a supreme sense. It is the knowledge *par excellence*. It is the only ground, the fundamental presupposition of all knowledge. All existing things, all objects of all thought receive their meaning from it. (सर्वविषयावभासनक्षम) With it there is all light, without it all darkness. Here are a few very remarkable passages in which Shankara lays it down in no ambiguous terms that Atman is the only reliable, the only available, the only intelligible basis of all our world of knowledge and action. Far from being an unknown quantity, of which we cannot say even that 'it exists' or that 'it does not exist', it is the very core, the very centre and source of all existence and all knowledge. " The existence of *Brahman* is known on the ground of its being the Self of everyone. For everyone is conscious of the existence of (his) Self, and never thinks ' I am not '. If the existence of the Self were not known, everyone would think ' I am not '." [61] " It is impossible to deny the Self, because he who denies it is the Self. The possible objection that there is no reason to maintain that the soul is known from the Upanishads only, since it is the object of self-consciousness, is refuted by the fact that the soul of which the Upanishads treat is merely the witness of that (i. e. of the object of self-consciousness, viz. the jiwatman). For neither from that part of the Veda which enjoins works nor from reasoning, anybody apprehends that soul which, different from the agent that is the object of self-consciousness, merely witnesses it...Hence it can neither be denied nor be represented as the mere

---

61. S. B. I. 17

compliment of injunctions; for of that very person who might deny it, it is the Self. And as it is the Self of all, it can neither be striven after nor avoided." [62] "The Self as being the abode of energy that acts through the means of right knowledge, is itself established previously to that energy. And to refute such a self-established entity is impossible. An adventitious thing, indeed, may be refuted, but not that which is the essential nature (of him who attempts the refutation); for it is the essential nature of him who refutes it. The heat of fire is not refuted (i. e. sublated) by fire itself."[63] An analysis of the contents of our ordinary consciousness shows us that the deepest, the most ineradicable, the most constant element in it is the idea of Self. Everyone feels that the most intimate part of his nature, the very centre of his being lies in this idea of Self. The consciousness of Self is, in fact, the one thing, of which we are absolutely sure. It is the very rock of our certitude. No reason-

---

62. S. B. I. 4. 4. 63. S. B. II. 3. 7.

ing however subtle or penetrating can explain away this fundamental fact of our nature, in the innermost recesses of our being, the one solid fact which stands firm and unshakable in the midst of all storms, which gives us the very sure guarantee that is required. We may go on doubting the existence and validity of every part of mind and nature, but we cannot doubt the doubter away. Such propositions as ' I doubt the existence of my being,' or ' I do not exist' carry within themselves their own refutation. The fact of I-ness, of self-consciousnesss is presupposed in either proposition. In fact, any attempt to charm away the I-ness is foredoomed to failure. A single thought, a single word, a single movement of head or heart is sufficient to destroy absolute scepticism. Even a dumb, speechless scepticism is an impossible attitude of mind. Bergson has very ably proved that the idea of pure nothingness is a pseudo-idea, that in its very nature it is an absurdity. We cannot either picture or conceive such a thing as absolute annihilation, absolute void or absolute nothingness. An irreducible minimum of consciousness persistently remains, permanently thwarting our endeavours to leap beyond the shadow of our thought. This residue of consciousness and reality can never be conjured away by any legerdemain, any trick of logic. Shankara's philosophy takes its stand upon this fact of facts, this eternal bedrock of reality, and his position thus is an impregnable one and no attacks from any quarter can dislodge it from this.

Thus we see that Shankara is right in maintaining that no proof can demonstrate the existence of the Absolute. The Absolute frustrates all attempts of logic to deduce or to refute its being. But the fact that it is out-side and above reason does not mean that it is contrary to reason. It is neither contradictory nor absurd. It is above reason in the sense that reason cannot catch its secret or penetrate its being. Yet it is not irrational, because it is the very source of reason, the very ground of logic, the very presupposition of knowledge, the one supreme condition which makes reason, logic, knowledge possible. It cannot be demonstrated by any proof, because all proofs assume its existence. "It is upon Self that the whole structure of proof is based; hence the Self itself is established previous to all such proofs."[64] The self-consciousness thus is the central fact in the epistemology of Shankara and must be very clearly and firmly grasped, for any tolerably adequate understanding of his system. Here at any rate the test of the inconceivability of the opposite is quite appropriate and so it is vigorously applied to establish the fundamental position of Shankara's system.

But it would be a feeble conclusion to say that the supreme Reality is known to us merely on the above epistemological basis. The inconceivability of the opposite is a very good test to establish the existence of Reality.

---

[64]. S. B. II. 3. 7.

But it is after all the logician's test. It cannot permanently satisfy us. Are we merely to say that all we can know about the Absolute is, that it is the one condition which makes all thought possible and any refutation of it is logically impossible ? Again, there is the psychological proof given in the first of the above quotations namely, the consciousness that everybody feels that he exists. But the idea of 'I' is a mere form without content. What is this ego ? How are we to conceive its nature ? Here Shankara rises above all the logical, the psychological and the epistemological proofs. It is not sufficient to conceive the possibility of the Absolute or to think of it as the supreme presupposition of all knowledge, or to conceive it as pure self-consciousness, the I which accompanies every act of thought or speech. It is possible to comprehend the Absolute as fully as we comprehend anything in the world; or further, we may have a fuller and more concrete view of Reality than we can have of any item in the Reality. We have got in intuition the possibility of having a first-hand view of Reality, of seeing the Absolute face to face, or realising it with all the fulness of which our nature is capable. In this way we have not merely an outside glimpse into the Reality; we have capacity of penetrating the very centre of being and graspsing it thence. This is the highest ground upon which all our knowledge of Reality is based. We can have immediate experience, direct realization of the Absolute. The intuition of the Absolute resembles perception rather than conception. It is as inevitable, as direct, as absolute as perception. It forces itself irresistibly on our consciousness. There can be no scope for doubt, hesitation, option 'this or that' in this act of realization. Reality as soon as it rises into view carries its conviction about itself; it lays hold upon our nature with absolute violence. It is objective certainty we attain and not subjective assurance, or rather it is absolute certitude, and neither subjective nor objective assurance which we get. In fact,

Reality overwhelms us so much that there is no possibility of our resisting its influence or escaping its sway. Even the I and thou, the subject and object of our ordinary experience completely vanish and such terms as knowledge or even intuition become meaningless. Thus in strict truth, we cannot even say in intuition we possess an organ of experiencing the Absolute. For such language though definite from the standpoint of thought, loses its meaning when we try to view it from the point of view of Reality itself.

The following passage sets forth the appropriateness of intuition for the knowledge of *Brahman*. " Scripture texts etc. are not, in the enquiry into *Brahman*, the only means of knowledge as they are in the enquiry into active duty; but scriptural texts on the one hand, and intuition on the other hand, are to be had recourse to according to the occasion; firstly, because intuition is the final result of the enquiry into *Brahman*; secondly, because the object of the enquiry is an existing (accomplished) substance."65 Again it is stated that *Brahman* is an accomplished entity and hence there is scope for the employment of means of right knowledge other than Shrutis. And the knowledge of *Brahman*...terminates in a perception (intuition of *Brahman*). Its effects are seen (but the effects of religious duties are not seen).66 " The fruit of complete knowledge springs up at the moment when complete knowledge is attained."67 " अनुभवावसानं तु ज्ञानफलम् " " The result of knowledge of *Brahman* is experienced by means of intuition; for the Shruti says ' The *Brahman* which is present to intuition; not hidden.' "68 Intuition is thus the goal of all aspirants after release; as long as it is not reached, all knowledge is ineffective.69 विज्ञान is often paraphrased by अनुभव by Shankara in his Commentary on the Gita.70

---

65. S. B. I. 1. 2.
66. S. B. II. 1. 4.   67. S. B. II. 1. 4.
68. S. B. I. 4. 14.   69 S. B. III. 3. 32.
70. Bg. C. VI. 8.; VII. 2. etc.

Intuition resembles perception in as much as both have to deal with accomplished object (भूतवस्तु or परिनिष्पन्नवस्तु); in both cases contact is direct; there is scope for criteria other than Shrutis; the result is immediately seen; there is no scope for doubt; the subjective factor is inoperative and the object makes itself felt. "No option is possible as to whether a substance is to be thus or thus, is to be or not to be. All option depends upon the notions of man, but the knowledge of the real nature of a thing depends only on the thing itself. For the idea with regard to a post—'this is a post or a man or something else' is not knowledge of truth; the two ideas, 'it is a man or something else' being false and only the third idea, 'it is a post', which depends on the thing itself, falling under the head of true knowledge. Thus true knowledge of all existing things depends on the things themselves and the knowledge of *Brahman* also depends altogether on the thing i. e. *Brahman* itself."[71]

---

71. S. B. I. 1. 2; III. 2. 21. etc,

"The fundamental texts about *Brahman* merely instruct man, instruction being their immediate result. The case is analogous to that of information regarding objects of sense which ensues as soon as objects are approximated to the senses."[72] Intuition resembles in some respects reasoning more than the holy tradition. "Reasoning which enables us to infer something not actually perceived in consequence of its having a certain equality of attributes with what is actually perceived, stands nearer to intuition than Shruti which conveys its sense by tradition only."[73] Practical exercises of Yoga or Bhakti are often recommended to bring about intuition of *Brahman*. Meditation is to be practised till a beatific vision flashes upon the soul.[74] Yoga is directed to be the means of attaining the cognition of *Brahman*. "The wise man should restrain the activity of the outer organs such as speech etc. and abide within the mind only: he should further restrain

---

72. S. B. I. 1. 1.   73. S. B. II. 1. 4.
74. S.B. IV. 1. 1.

the mind which is intent on doubtful external objects within intelligence, whose characteristic mark is decision recognising that indecision is evil; he should further restrain intelligence within the great Self i. e. the individual soul; he should finally fix the great Self on the calm Self i. e. the highest Self."75 The value of the factor of devotion is also recognised in this connection. " At the time of ecstatic vision the Yogin sees the unevolved Self, free from all plurality. By ' ecstatic vision ' we mean the presentation before the mind (of the highest Self) which is effected through meditation."76 The state of intuition is a ' unio mystica ' in which all duality ceases. (" निरस्तसमस्तप्रपंचम्; " " ज्ञाते द्वैतं न विद्यते ") It is characterised by cessation of intellectual doubts, or emotional agitation; it is a state of ecstatic peace, delightful repose.*

---

75. S. B. I. 4. 1.
76. S. B. III. 2. 24.

* भिद्यते हृदयग्रंथिः छिद्यन्ते सर्वसंशयाः ।
क्षीयन्ते चास्य कर्माणि तस्मिन्दृष्टे परावरे ॥

We have discussed the fact of intuition and the main features which characterise it. But how is it possible ? Is it by means of some supersensuous faculty that we cognise the Self, the Reality ? No; there is no necessity of invoking here either subconscious or superconscious organ of perception. The Atman or *Brahman* shines by its own nature. Its only evidence is sef-evidence. Its very nature is light. It is frequently called स्वयंज्योतिः or चैतन्यस्वरुप or स्वयंसिद्ध. The Atman knows itself; like the sun, it illuminates itself as well as other objects. It is the source, and centre of all light, illumination, knowledge. Thus, epistemology merges in ontology; the theory of knowledge merges in the theory of being; the two become entirely identical; all rational is real, all real is rational; there is one knowledge, one being; epistemologically, it may

---

* This is the characteristic difference between the intuition of Bergson and Shankara. There is no religious emotion present in the former at all; while in the latter it is that which colours all views.

be knowledge; ontologically it may be being. But two factors knowledge and being become one; all externality drops down; all duality disappears. " ज्ञाते द्वैतं न विद्यते "

III CONCLUSION.

Now the question arises as to the respective claims of reasoning and authority (or Shruti or revelation) in Shankara's theory of knowledge. This question is of very great importance inasmuch as upon the right view we arrive at with regard to it, depends the reputation of Shankara as a philosopher. He is run down as a mere theologian by many writers Eastern and Western, on the ground that he is guided throughout his works by the Vedas. Theology no doubt renders important services to us but it is largely dogmatic. It does not examine its own presuppositions. Philosophy, on the other hand, which wants to appeal to the world at large must be prepared to base its conclusions on an independent investigation into knowledge and reality in the dry light of reason. It takes nothing for granted and adopts assumptions only after proving their indespensability as assumptions. Philosophy in fact, is essentially rational. Shankaracharya's title to being a great philosopher, nay, a philosopher at all, must depend upon his taking his stand upon reason ultimately, and not on authority.

It must be admitted at the outset that with all orthodox schools of Hindu philosophy, the authority of the Shrutis is to a very great extent the very basis of truth. But this statement must be taken with qualifications; and further it was not altogether a disadvantage. In the first place, it was necessary for a Hindu thinker to show himself in fundamental agreement with the Shrutis, because the faith of the masses was firmly anchored upon this fact. It was altogether inadvisable in those days to unsettle the very foundations of religion and philosophy of the people. A philosopher in India, therefore, could hope to obtain the ear of the people, only by appealing to the Shrutis and it was also by this means that he could secure the organic coherence of philosophic speculation, from times immemorial. Another advantage which this procedure secured for the Hindu thought was that very happy blending of religion and philosophy, of metaphysics and life, which was one of the most attractive features of ancient Hindu life. A reciprocal influence was exercised by these two vital departments of human thought and conduct, and the result was a double one. Philosophy did not remain an academic activity of the few; it became a living force, a mighty tradition, a universal leaven among the people of all ranks and conditions. Religion in its turn developed its speculative side, it threw off many of its narrow, bigoted superstitions, anthropomorphic traits; it became in the hands of the educated Hindus one of the most refined and finished products of the joint operation of thought and feeling, of speculation and life. Again, the philosophical thought of the Upanishads, which became the source of the streams of metaphysical influences of varied type, was a body of the finest speculations ever known to man.

Dr. Deussen says: " An essential difference consists in modern philosophy in its fundamental character, even up to day—being a toilsome struggle, and a gradual shaking off of the fetters of mediaeval scholasticism,—while the Indian philosopher through all time has been the better, the more closely he has adhered to the basis laid down in the Vedic Upanishads. But in truth, this basis is also of on eminently philosophic character." Another point of very great importance in this connection is that in the eyes of the Hindu metaphysicians, the subject of metaphysics is of a unique type. The Absolute, by its very nature, could not be an object of either sense perception or of intellection. The ultimate Reality (*Brahman*) transcended our powers of thought and speech most completely. It could only be an object of intuition to the very highest and most accomplished sages and philosophers. This experience must be of a very rare type. The seers of the Upanishads came to a recognition of the greatest metaphysical truths not through reasoning merely, but through direct experience. The Upanishads, therefore, formed a symposium of the revelations of the direct immediate experiences of the Absolute, arrived at by the laborious processes of the highest and most cultured Rishis of many times and places. Hence if any human assistance can be conceived to exist in a matter of such a unique type, it must be the body of literature which contained the quintessence of human experience of various saints, working independently in different places and times, on subjects of such unique type as God and Soul, reality or unreality of Existence, and so on. It would be therefore no less absurd for a Hindu Metaphysician to discard altogether the basis of the Upanishads than for a modern philosophy to ignore absolutely and completely the whole course of philosophic development from Plato down to Hegel. A passion for originality or for the exercise of unfettered independence of the human intellect which ignores all the old wisdom altogether and tries to creat a philosophy *de novo* is a very shortsighted passion or rather a suicidal one. We do not know of any great philosopher who entirely cut himself adrift from the old moorings and started an entirely original system. Originality or freedom of reason does not exist in an independence of the past. In this respect, Plato and Aristotle, Kant and Hegel were no more original philosophers than Shankara and Ramanuja. On the other hand, the very greatness of these giants of human intellect consists in the fact they could assimilate their whole past more successfully than anyone else did. The dependence of the Hindu philosophers upon the Shrutis was to a great extent a dependence of this type. Shankara did not take bodily into his system everything that is to be found in the Upanishads, no more that Plato or Kant copied in their systems the features of the preceding philosophies only. The Shrutis in fact were collective wisdom of the most varied type; various theories and views were found there lying side by side. It was thus necessary for philosophers like Shankara and Ramanuja or for Kapila and Badarayana to typify those features of the Upanishadic thought which seemed to them fundamental and work them up into a rounded harmonious whole. In this way, these men could at once incorporate the thought and the spirit of the ancient wisdom, and yet maintain their position as completely independent and original thinkers.

Our conclusion, therefore, is that judged from the externals, Shankara's system appears to be more like the mediaeval schools or the jewish systems. But a detailed study of the fundamental positions of Shankara's system dissolves such an illusion. It was a necessity of his position which compelled him to support his system with theologic buttresses. But his system does not stand in need of any support. A few fundamental assumptions indeed, he inherited from previous thought. But these were not taken merely on the ground they were a part of the Shrutis. As a matter of fact, the Upanishads form a perfect symposium of speculation, in which support may be found for many conflicting views. Shankara took his stand on certain fundamental positions, because these appeared to him eminently reasonable; and this eminent reasonableness he tries to bring out fully. From the point of view of the strictly orthodox Hindu, he is concerned to show that he is in full agreement with the thought of the Shrutis. From the point of view of a philosopher, he is equally concerned to show that he addresses himself not to man's instinct for authority, but to his reason and to his deeper mystical experience. Like Hume, he exposes the fiction of a mere habitual belief in cause and effect. Like Kant, he is convinced that phenomena are mere appearances, that Reality is unknowable for intelligence. Like Bergson, he tries to show the intuitive basis of our highest knowledge. Like Hegel, he sees that the subject and object are one, that the real is the rational and the rational is real. It is our firm conviction, therefore, that Shankara has as much title to the name of philosopher as any of these brilliant thinkers. Dr. Deussen also agrees with this. He says : " Of the possibility here suggested of bringing in reflexion as an aid, our author makes a far more extensive use than might appear from these expressions. Since this side of Shankara's work, has for us the chief interest, we will, as far as possible, pass over his endless quotations from the Veda, but on the other hand, bend our whole attention to the philosophic reflexion. The perfection of the latter, as it meets us in Shankara's commentary may itself speak for the fact that we have here to do with a monument of Indian Antiquity not merely theological, but also in the highest degree philosophical. "

Shankara, we believe, represents a certain type of thought, a certain philosophical temperament which will continue to interest hundreds of thinkers of a similar cast. He has given to the world one of the greatest structures of thought ever reared by human intellect. It is a bold attempt at constructing a brilliant system, grasping in its wide sweep all reality and all knowledge. Elements of the greatest metaphysical value are there; elements whose worth will not die, as long as the metaphysical imagination of man will live. The system attempts to penetrate the very secret of being, to explain the ultimate nature of thought, to grasp the very kernel of Reality. It is a brilliant analysis of the Self, of the Self as the centre of man's cognitions, feelings, and volitions, and of the Self as the source of the intelligiblity of the outer world. It discovers man in God and God in man, soul in nature and nature in soul, subject in object and object in subject, and above all the Real in the Rational and the Rational in the Real.

Some Preliminary Announcements

of

THE GAEKWAD STUDIES

IN

RELIGION AND PHILOSOPHY

Edited by

ALBAN G. WIDGERY M.A.,

Professor of Philosophy and the Comparative Study of Religions, Baroda.

This Series is established with the sanction and financial support of the Government of His Highness the Maharajah Gaekwad of Baroda. The aim is to provide an opportunity for the publication of works on religious and philosophical subjects. Some of the volumes will be more popular and some more technical in nature. Only books written in the tolerant spirit of genuine scholarship will be included.

The Manager,
THE COLLEGE, BARODA.

THE GAEKWAD STUDIES IN RELIGION AND PHILOSOPHY

First issues:

Personality and Atonement. By the Editor.

Human Needs and The Justification of Religions Beliefs. By the Editor.

The Heart of the Bhagavatgita. By Lingesha Mahabhagavat.

Zoroastrian Ethics. By M. A. Buch.

Kant and S'ankaracharya. Prof. C. G. Bhate, Poona.

Selections from Al-Ghassali. By Professor Syed Nawab Ali.

The Doctrine of Karma. A Volume of Essays by various writers.

Immortality and Other Essays. By the Editor.

The Comparative Study of Religions. By the Editor.

A Buddhist Bibliography. By various scholars.

A Chronology and Bibliography of Muslim Literature on Religion and Philosophy. By Professor M. Jamil ur Rehman and F. S. Gilani, M. A.

Some Modern Religious Movements. By various writers.

Jesus. By the Editor.

Goods and Bads: Outlines of a Philosophy of Life. By the Editor.

HUMAN NEEDS
AND
THE JUSTIFICATION OF RELIGIOUS BELIEFS

The Burney Prize Essay Cambridge 1909

and

PERSONALITY AND ATONEMENT

Essays in the Philosophy of Religion.

by

ALBAN G. WIDGERY

Cloth : Six Rupees

THE HEART OF THE BHAGAVAD-GITA

BY

His Holiness S'ri Vidya S'ankara Bharati Swami, Jagadguru S'ankaracharya of Karvir Pitha.

In this book one of the most enlightened leaders of Modern Hindu religious life discusses the important and ever interesting question : "What is the value of the Gita as a guide to practical life?" It should be read by all educated Hindus and by all non-Hindus who wish to know the religious attitude of a prominent Hindu scholar and devotee.

The Manager,
THE COLLEGE, BARODA.

IMMORTALITY
AND OTHER ESSAYS
BY
ALBAN G. WIDGERY

Paper covers : Two rupees
Cloth : Three rupees.

The Manager,
THE COLLEGE, BARODA.

THE CONFUTATION OF ATHEISM
Translated by
VALI MOHAMMED CHHAGANBHAI MOMIN.

This short treatise which comes down from the sixth Imam, Hazrat Imam Jafar-us-Sadak, should prove of great interest to all Muslims. It will attract others also by the beauty of its style and the remarkable likeness it bears to the arguments of Bishop Butler in his *Analogy of Religion*.

Fourteen annas, post free.

The Manager,
THE COLLEGE, BARODA.

ZOROASTRIAN ETHICS

BY

MAGANLAL A. BUCH M. A.,

Fellow of the Seminar for the Comparative Study of Religions, Baroda.

CONTENTS

Introduction.
Bibliography.

PART I

I. The Available Zoroastrian Literature.
II. The Historical and Social Conditions.
III. Psychological Conceptions.

PART II

IV. The General Moral Attitude.
V. The Value of Life : Industry and Indolence.
VI. Truthfulness and Deceit : Purity and Impurity.
VII. The Ethics of Sex Relations.
VIII. Benevolence : other Vices and Virtues.
IX. The Ethical in Legal References in Zoroastrian Literature.
X. Theological and Metaphysical Conceptions.
Index.

Paper covers : Two Rupees.
Cloth covers : Three Rupees.

The Manager,
THE COLLEGE, BARODA.

In the Press

THE COMPARATIVE STUDY OF RELIGIONS
A Systematic Survey

By

ALBAN G. WIDGERY M A.,

Professor of Philosophy and the Comparative Study of Religions, Baroda.

CONTENTS.

INTRODUCTION: Scientific Theology and the Comparative Study of Religions

I. The Sources and Nature of Religious Truth.
II. Supernatural Beings, Good and Bad.
III. The Soul: its Nature, Origin, and Destiny.
IV. Sin and Suffering: Salvation and Redemption.
V. Religious Practices.
VI. The Emotional Attitudes and Religious Ideals.

Appendices; Maps; Illustrations; Bibliography; and Index.

This volume is meant to be a systematic introduction to the subject. Much of the technical detail being in the form of notes the book is thus adapted to the general reader as well as to the needs of students.

Cloth, superior paper Rs. 12.; 15-s. 0d.
Cloth, ordinary paper Rs. 10.; 12-s. 6d.

The Manager,
THE COLLEGE, BARODA.

In preparation

An important volume of Essays on

THE DOCTRINE OF KARMA

By

Representatives of the different great religions.

The purpose of the volume is to present for comparison the views of certain writers of distinction from the different religions upon the theory that the suffering and happiness of the individual is due solely to his own action, past or present.

Some Contributors

Shams-ul-Ulama J. J. Modi, C. I. E., Ph. D.,
The Very Rev. Hastings Rashdall, D. Lit ; D.C.L.
S. Khuda Buksch, M. A., B. C. L., (Oxon.)
Champat Rai Jain, Author of *The Key of Knowledge*
Israel Abrahams, D. Lit.
Alban G. Widgery M. A. (Cantab.)

The Manager,
THE COLLEGE, BARODA.

In preparation by Various Scholars

A BUDDHIST BIBLIOGRAPHY

CONTENTS

Preface. *Introduction.*

BOOK I.

I. Buddhist Literature in Pali with translations, Commentaries, and References to specific works in European Languages.

II. Buddhist Literature in Sanskrit with translations, Commentaries, and References to specific works in European Languages.

III. References to Buddhism in non-Buddhist Sanskrit Literature.

IV. Buddhism in General with special References to Buddhist Doctrine and Practice in European Languages.

BOOK II.

I. Buddhism in India (works in European Languages only).

II. Buddhism in Ceylon.

III. Buddhism in Burma.

IV. Buddhism in Malay and Java.

V. Buddhism in Siam and Cambodia.

VI. Buddhism in Himalayan Tracts.

VII. Buddhism in Tibet.

VIII. Buddhism in Central Asia and Mongolia.

IX. Buddhism in China. X. Buddhism in Korea.

XI. Buddhism in Japan.

Appendices, Maps, Indices.

The Manager,
THE COLLEGE, BARODA.

Lightning Source UK Ltd.
Milton Keynes UK
UKOW02f2147130114

224542UK00012B/613/P